I0816102

THE PITTSBURGH PENGUINS

AN ILLUSTRATED TIMELINE

Mario Lemieux hoists the Stanley Cup as the Penguins celebrate their second straight championship after defeating the Chicago Blackhawks, June 1, 1992.
COURTESY OF GETTY IMAGES

THE PITTSBURGH PENGUINS

AN ILLUSTRATED TIMELINE

DAVE MOLINARI

Reedy Press
PO Box 5131
St. Louis, MO 63139, USA
www.reedypress.com

Library of Congress Control Number: 2025936217

ISBN: 9781681066110

Cover and Interior Design: Eric Marquard

All front cover images courtesy of Getty Images. All back cover images courtesy of Getty Images. All interior photos courtesy of Getty Images unless otherwise noted.

Printed in Canada
25 26 27 28 29 5 4 3 2 1

DEDICATION

To Kelsey, Jeremy, and Jessica for their support and sacrifices. And to the coworkers, colleagues, and competitors who have pushed me throughout my career.

CONTENTS

Mario Lemieux's first set of NHL teammates included numerous holdovers from previous seasons.
COURTESY OF GETTY IMAGES

Mario Lemieux scored one of the iconic goals in team history during the 1991 Stanley Cup Final against Minnesota.
COURTESY OF GETTY IMAGES

The Penguins' sweep of Chicago in the 1992 Cup Final gave them back-to-back championships.
COURTESY OF GETTY IMAGES

The Civic Arena, with its novel shape and retractable roof, added a unique element to the Pittsburgh skyline. COURTESY OF GETTY IMAGES

Mario Lemieux and Wayne Gretzky squared off in the 1990 All-Star Game, the only time it's been held in Pittsburgh.
COURTESY OF GETTY IMAGES

INTRODUCTION

THE PITTSBURGH PENGUINS have been a lot of things since they entered the National Hockey League in 1967. Hapless, hopeless, habitual losers. Repeat champions. Chronically challenged. Extraordinarily talented. Almost everything at one time or another, it seems, except boring. They've been through multiple bankruptcies and endured nearly a quarter century during which nearly all of their high points during the playoffs came in valiant defeats. They've also had once-in-a-lifetime talents—guys like Mario Lemieux and Sidney Crosby, Jaromir Jagr and Evgeni Malkin—turn up on their depth chart with astonishing regularity for the past four decades.

As one who has followed the Penguins since they joined the NHL and has covered them since the summer of 1983—first for *The Pittsburgh Press*, then the *Pittsburgh Post-Gazette* and a pair of websites—I've had a front-row seat to much that the franchise has endured, and much that it has accomplished. It's been fascinating to witness and to relive while working on this book.

Although the Penguins weren't necessarily always worth watching, there always was something to see with them. There's no reason to believe that will change anytime soon, which means there is plenty on which to look back, and just as much to see in the future.

The NHL's 1967 expansion pitted the Penguins against established clubs like the Detroit Red Wings.
COURTESY OF GETTY IMAGES

The Penguins moved into their new home, the Consol Energy Center, in the fall of 2010.
COURTESY OF GETTY IMAGES

ACKNOWLEDGMENTS

ONE OF THE ADVANTAGES to being a longtime beat writer when taking on a project like identifying the most memorable moments and people of a franchise that's been around for more than 50 years is having witnessed most of the events and known most of the participants. Still, memories can fade and even become distorted over time, so having resources that can verify details of events in the distant past is invaluable.

The online archives of *The Pittsburgh Press* (via newspapers.com) and the *Pittsburgh Post-Gazette* (thank you, Mt. Lebanon Public Library) were especially helpful, because those publications covered the Penguins daily. (And while the *Press* was put out of business at the end of 1992, the *Post-Gazette* continues to man the Penguins beat.) Information also was gleaned from a number of other sources, from the *New York Times* to *Pittsburgh Hockey Now*, the Associated Press, and the *Los Angeles Times*. All helped to plug informational voids in some of the entries in this book.

Another inestimable asset was the Pittsburgh Penguins' archives of score sheets. The information those contain has evolved over the years—they started with the most basic data and have grown to include things like ice time and blocked shots, among many others—but all were helpful in confirming dates, times, stats, and other details.

The Penguins are 2-0 against the Sabres in the playoffs, with both series-clinching wins coming in overtime in Buffalo.
COURTESY OF GETTY IMAGES

Steelers owner Art Rooney played a prominent role in Pittsburgh getting an NHL team.
COURTESY OF GETTY IMAGES

JUNE 5, 1967

A FRANCHISE IS BORN

THE PITTSBURGH PENGUINS officially joined the National Hockey League, which doubled in size from its Original Six by adding franchises in Pittsburgh, Minnesota, St. Louis, Philadelphia, Los Angeles, and Oakland. Pittsburgh Steelers owner Art Rooney was one of many investors in the team and played an important behind-the-scenes role in the city getting a club. The NHL's expansion plan called for two new teams in the West, two in the Midwest, and two in the East. Five of those slots already were filled, and Pittsburgh was competing with Buffalo to get the final opening. "The Buffalo group went all-out to pick off the sixth franchise," said state senator Jack McGregor, who headed the Pittsburgh group seeking to land a team. McGregor recruited Rooney to lobby Bruce Norris, who owned the Detroit Red Wings, and his brother Jim, who owned the Chicago Blackhawks, to not only back the Penguins, but to convince the league's other owners to do so. "I'll never forget Art calling each [of the Norris

brothers] from his New York City hotel room, in my presence," McGregor said. "He said to each, 'You owe this to me. You cannot put Buffalo ahead of Pittsburgh. It would be personally embarrassing to me if you did.'" Rooney's effort paid off, as both of the Norris brothers, as well as the owners of the Montreal Canadiens (David Molson) and New York Rangers (William Jennings) voted in favor of giving Pittsburgh a team. McGregor and Peter Block were the primary owners, each holding 12.5 percent of the club. They and their partners paid $2.5 million for the franchise, and McGregor served as the club's first president and chief executive officer.

JUNE 5, 1967

WHAT'S IN A NAME?

WITH PITTSBURGH'S formal entry into the NHL, their unlikely nickname Penguins was added to the league's lexicon. There had been considerable sentiment to retain the name carried by Pittsburgh's American Hockey League franchise, the Hornets, which had won the league championship in its final season of existence. But Jack Riley, general manager of the city's new NHL club, later offered a good explanation for not doing so. "We thought about keeping the Hornets nickname," he said. "But we weren't sure that an NHL expansion team could deliver for the loyal locals." Mellon National Bank, the Hockey Club of Pittsburgh, and the *Pittsburgh Post-Gazette* conducted a name-the-team contest that attracted 26,400 entries, ranging from the Pioneers to the Golden Triangles and from the Queens to the Zeniths. When the voting ended, 716 people had proposed calling the team the Penguins and part-owner Peter Block agreed that the name seemed like a natural. "The penguin lives on ice," he said. "Hockey players make their living on ice. And then there is the nickname of 'Big Igloo,' which has become a part of the Civic Arena."

This is the original version of the Penguins' logo, which has had numerous iterations over the years.
© PITTSBURGH PENGUINS

Hank Bassen was the losing goalie in the Penguins' NHL debut, a 2-1 defeat by Montreal at the Civic Arena.
© PITTSBURGH PENGUINS

OCTOBER 11, 1967

LET THE GAMES BEGIN

THE PENGUINS made their on-ice NHL debut with a 2–1 loss to Montreal at the Civic Arena. Future Hall of Famer Andy Bathgate, who had been claimed from the New York Rangers in the expansion draft, scored for Pittsburgh, but it was not enough to counter goals by J.C. Tremblay and Jean Beliveau of the Canadiens. "Gee, it would have been nice [to defeat the Canadiens]," Penguins coach Red Sullivan said afterward. Penguins goalie Hank Bassen stopped 33 of 35 shots, while Montreal goalie Rogie Vachon turned aside 34. "I never saw our team so nervous," Canadiens coach Toe Blake said. "We must have given them the puck . . . I don't know how many times. . . . I tell you, I'm very happy to get out of here with two points." The game attracted a crowd of 9,307, well below the building's capacity of 12,580. Beliveau's goal was the 400th in his career. "It's a lot if you go for sentiment, 400 is," he said. "But I never bother too much. Every year when I start a new season, I have no fixed number. I just try as good as possible and don't think about that." He scored number 400 by converting the rebound of a John Ferguson shot from close range, although Bassen said he didn't have a reasonable opportunity to make the stop. "Somebody [from Montreal] was sitting on me," he said. "That's why I was complaining to the ref [John Ashley]. How was I supposed to get up?"

OCTOBER 13, 1967

ONE STEP FORWARD

THE FIRST WIN in franchise history came against a club that would become the Penguins' most bitter rival in their early years, St. Louis. Ab McDonald, Art Stratton, and Earl Ingarfield scored for Pittsburgh in what would go down as its first-ever victory. Stratton's power-play goal at 17:51 of the second period broke a 1–1 tie and earned a footnote in team annals as the Penguins' first game winner. Stratton, who had been the leading scorer and MVP in the American Hockey League in 1964–65, scored on Blues rookie goalie Seth Martin, off assists from Keith McCreary and Gene Ubriaco. Before joining the Penguins, Stratton had spent the previous two seasons in St. Louis where, as a farmhand of the Chicago Blackhawks, he labored for the Central Professional Hockey League's St. Louis Braves. Although Martin, who turned aside 32 shots, took the loss, he and Penguins goalie Hank Bassen, who finished with 37 saves, both turned in strong performances. "If it wasn't for that kid in goal for St. Louis in the second period, we would have had two or three more goals," Penguins coach Red Sullivan said.

The Penguins claimed Earl Ingarfield from the New York Rangers in the 1967 expansion draft.
COURTESY OF GETTY IMAGES

OCTOBER 18, 1967

THAT DIDN'T TAKE LONG

ANDY BATHGATE, in the latter stages of his Hall of Fame career, recorded the first hat trick in franchise history, scoring all three of the Penguins' goals in a 3–3 tie with the Minnesota North Stars at the Civic Arena. Bathgate got two of his goals against Cesare Maniago and the other on Gary Bauman, and he did it in just the team's fourth game in the league. While the North Stars didn't have an answer for Bathgate on the ice, Minnesota coach Wren Blair had an interesting observation about Bathgate after the final buzzer. "I don't watch the other team," he said. "I only have time to watch my players. Did he play?" While Bathgate obviously did his part—and a lot more—in this game, Penguins coach Red Sullivan was visibly displeased with what he got (or, more to the point, didn't get) from some of his other veterans against the North Stars. "It took us 40 minutes to get started," he said. "Some of these guys feel all they've got to do is throw their stick on the ice. And I'm talking about the guys I figure should be carrying the club. They'd better get on the ball, I'll tell you that." Bathgate, whose goals gave him five for the season, one more than Chicago goal-scorer extraordinaire Bobby Hull at that early juncture, was an obvious exception. If there was any consolation for the Penguins, it was that only 3,885 witnesses were on hand for the game.

Andy Bathgate scored 20 goals for the Penguins during their inaugural season in the NHL.
COURTESY OF GETTY IMAGES

Sellout crowds were rare in the Penguins' early years, even when Original Six clubs like Detroit came to town.
COURTESY OF GETTY IMAGES

FEBRUARY 3, 1968

THE GANG'S ALL HERE

ALTHOUGH IT would be decades before the Penguins set an NHL record by selling out 633 consecutive games, they attracted the first capacity crowd at home in team history when a standing-room crowd of 12,563 showed up at the Civic Arena for a 3–3 tie with Toronto. It was the third consecutive Saturday on which Pittsburgh set a single-game attendance record. Why so many fans showed up for this game never will be known, but perhaps they knew Pittsburgh had a chance to become the first expansion team to take a season series from an Original Six club. The tie achieved that, giving the Penguins a 2–1–1 mark against the Maple Leafs. That outcome didn't seem likely in the first period, when Frank Mahovlich scored a pair of unanswered goals for Toronto. But Gene Ubriaco, recently recalled from the Penguins' farm team in Baltimore, triggered Pittsburgh's comeback when he punched an Andy Bathgate pass past Toronto goalie Johnny Bowers 71 seconds into the middle period and Ab McDonald converted a Val Fonteyne rebound at 16:13 to tie the game. Toronto countered quickly, as Dave Keon deflected a Mahovlich feed past Penguins goalie Les Binkley just 42 seconds later, but McDonald got his second of the game at 4:52 of the third to close out the scoring—and to make coach Red Sullivan a happy man. "They couldn't have given me any more than they did," he said. "That was a real hockey game tonight. There were bodies all over the ice."

Coach Red Kelly guided the Penguins to their first appearance in the Stanley Cup playoffs. COURTESY OF GETTY IMAGES

APRIL 1, 1970

WELCOME TO THE PLAYOFFS

THE SIX TEAMS that entered the NHL in the 1967 expansion came in with modest expectations and objectives; simply qualifying for the playoffs was the ceiling for most of them. Even that exceeded the Penguins' grasp during their first two seasons, however, so when they beat Philadelphia, 4–1 at the Civic Arena to secure second place in the West Division and a berth in the postseason, it was a cause for celebration—and not only because each player earned a $1,250 bonus. "What a difference a year makes," defenseman Bob Woytowich said. "A year ago at this time, we had our bags packed for home." Although equipment manager Ken Carson was so excited by their accomplishment that he scrawled "We're No. 2" on a blackboard in the locker room, some of the players insisted that they had known the team was capable of finishing high in the division. "I told my parents and friends at the beginning of the season that we would finish first or second," rookie center Michel Briere said. "I thought we had a lot of good hockey players and the best coach in the league." That would be Red Kelly, who had been a Hall of Fame player and who had replaced Red Sullivan behind the bench after the Penguins finished fifth in the West in each of their first two seasons. The outcome of the Philadelphia game was in doubt until the final minute, when Bob Blackburn and Dean Prentice scored empty-net goals. Jean Pronovost's second-period goal on Philadelphia's Bernie Parent held up as the game winner and allowed him to meet a key personal objective. "It was just in my mind to get 20 goals," he said. "No matter what happened."

APRIL 8, 1970

SEALS OF DISAPPROVAL

IT TOOK the Penguins three years to get into the Stanley Cup playoffs, but only one game to be mired in their first postseason controversy. Immediately after the Penguins' 2–1 victory over the Oakland Seals in their Round 1 opener, Seals officials protested that Penguins winger Glen Sather had been in goalie Gary Smith's crease when Nick Harbaruk knocked in a Wally Boyer rebound at 12:46 of the third period for what proved to be the game winner. "I saw the whole side of the net open," Harbaruk said. "I would have kicked myself if I'd missed that. I've missed those shots before, but not now." Had Sather been deemed guilty of being in the crease when Harbaruk scored, it would have been a clear violation of NHL rules and the goal would have been waved off. The Seals didn't deny that defenseman Bert Marshall had put Sather in the crease, but contended that detail didn't matter. "There's no question that our guy pushed him in the crease," Oakland GM Frank Selke said. "But he didn't hold him there. The player is supposed to make an effort to get out." The Penguins, predictably, were having none of it. "If they didn't want [Sather] in there, why did they hit him?" coach Red Kelly said. Seals executives appealed to NHL representative Bill van Deelan to get the Penguins to give Oakland their game film, but that request was rejected out of hand. "We don't loan our film," Kelly said.

JANUARY 26, 1971

THERE WAS AN APPS FOR THAT

ONE OF the least popular personnel moves during the Penguins' early years turned out to be one of the most important—and productive. GM Jack Riley sent gritty winger Glen (Slats) Sather to the New York Rangers for center Syl Apps and a player to be named later (defenseman Shelson Kannegiesser). One skeptical fan draped a "Why Slats?" banner in the Civic Arena when the Penguins faced Toronto there the next night. Apps provided an answer by scoring the game-winning goal and setting up another in a 3–1 Penguins victory. Those were the first two of 500 points he would put up in 495 regular-season games with Pittsburgh, many of which he spent in the middle of what came to be known as the Century Line, with Jean Pronovost and Lowell MacDonald on the wings. MacDonald wasn't in the Penguins' lineup when Apps made his Penguins debut the night after the trade, but Apps made an excellent first impression, regardless. Especially with his second-period goal, which became the game winner. "Most beautiful goal I've seen in a long time," coach Red Kelly said. "He gave [goalie Jacques] Plante [a lunge to the right], and then [a lunge to the left] and you could see Plante thinking, 'I've got him.' So Plante puts his stick out and then the kid dekes him again and I tell you, it just made bubbles inside. Ho-ho. First time I've chuckled all year." The Penguins would go on to sweep the best-of-seven series from the Seals, with Michel Briere clinching the series with an overtime goal in Game 4.

Syl Apps, who centered the Century Line, was one of the Penguins' earliest stars.
COURTESY OF GETTY IMAGES

Goalie Al Smith stopped pucks and, occasionally, started mayhem during his days with the Penguins. COURTESY OF GETTY IMAGES

APRIL 4, 1971

A BLACK-AND-BLUES RIVALRY

HE WAS known to some as "Battlin' Al Smith," and he lived up to that moniker in a game against the archrival Blues, trading punches with St. Louis defenseman Bob Plager—who, like his brother Barclay, was wildly unpopular in Pittsburgh—in the first period of a 1–1 tie at the Civic Arena. Smith and Plager had at it at center ice, but only after Smith had taken a brief timeout to go to the bench to remove his goaltending equipment. Smith was assessed a roughing minor, fighting major, and game misconduct for his trouble, while Plager got a charging minor, fighting major, and game misconduct. Their confrontation came at 18:43 of the opening period, which had already featured some unpleasant exchanges between the teams. Bob Plager skated into Smith, who had made a save on St. Louis's Jim Roberts and was covering the puck while on his hands and knees in the crease. The two were separated twice but managed to get back together and renew hostilities. Penguins defenseman Dunc McCallum and Noel Picard of the Blues squared off at the same time Smith and Plager were having at it, although Smith–Plager definitely was the headliner, and referee Ron Wicks declared the period to be over, with the 77 seconds remaining added to the start of the second period. For the night, Wicks handed out 88 minutes in penalties—50 of them to St. Louis—including 61 in that raucous first period. Largely overlooked because of all of the mayhem in this regular-season finale was that the tie dropped the Penguins into sixth place in the seven-team West Division.

APRIL 2, 1972

MIRACLE AT THE AUD

THE PENGUINS' 6–2 victory over St. Louis at the Civic Arena in the regular-season finale wouldn't have been particularly memorable—if Buffalo's Gerry Meehan hadn't beaten Philadelphia goalie Doug Favell with a long-distance shot with only four seconds remaining in regulation at Memorial Auditorium to give the Sabres a 3–2 win. That handed the Penguins fourth place in the West Division and the final berth in the Stanley Cup playoffs, a spot that would have gone to the Flyers if not for Meehan. Many in the crowd at the Civic Arena were following events in Buffalo on transistor radios, with a predictable outburst of joy when the Sabres won. And anyone in attendance who hadn't gotten word of the Flyers' fate was quickly informed when public-address man Beckley Smith announced it. The Penguins still had to win their game against the Blues to take advantage of Philadelphia's misfortune, but they had control of it long before Meehan scored. After Jim Roberts had staked St. Louis to a 1–0 lead, the Penguins got goals from Nick Harbaruk, Greg Polis, Eddie Shack, and Ron Schock to go comfortably in front. While Meehan's heroics gave the Penguins the final nudge they needed to appear in the playoffs for the second time in franchise history, Pittsburgh had staged a pretty impressive comeback the night before in Philadelphia to make the final games of the season—the one in Pittsburgh, as well as the one at the Aud—meaningful. They had rallied from a 4–2 deficit in the third period, earning a tie when Polis scored with 46 seconds to go in regulation.

Buffalo's Gerry Meehan made himself a cult hero in Pittsburgh by scoring a season-saving goal against Philadelphia. COURTESY OF GETTY IMAGES

APRIL 13, 1971

A STAR DIMS FAR TOO SOON

MICHEL BRIERE, who was envisioned as the first homegrown superstar in Penguins history, died of injuries sustained in an auto accident in his native Quebec on May 15, 1970. He would become the first Pittsburgh player to have his number retired, and held the distinction of being the only one so honored until Mario Lemieux's number 66 was raised at Mellon Arena more than a quarter century later. Briere was driving his Mercury Cougar on the Trans-Canada Highway near Malartic, Quebec, when the car flipped as he was going around a bend. He was thrown from the vehicle and suffered major head injuries that ultimately proved to be fatal despite four surgeries on his brain. Ken Carson, then the Penguins' equipment manager and trainer, took Briere's equipment bag with him to every game the team played during the 1970–71 season. Carson was part of a six-member contingent of Penguins officials—GM Jack Riley and coach Red Kelly also were in the group—that attended Briere's funeral, and a memorial service for Briere subsequently was held at St. Paul's Cathedral in Pittsburgh. In 2024, the Penguins would invite members of Briere's family to attend the ceremony during which Jaromir Jagr's number 68 was retired, making him just the third player in franchise history to be so honored.

Michel Briere established himself as a budding superstar during his only season in Pittsburgh. COURTESY OF GETTY IMAGES

APRIL 9, 1972

HORRIBLE NIGHT FOR HORTON

THERE WAS no question that the Penguins were overmatched and outclassed when paired with Chicago in their opening-round playoff series. They had finished 41 points behind the Blackhawks during the regular season, and Chicago's lineup was studded with future Hall of Famers like Bobby Hull, Stan Mikita, and Tony Esposito. The Penguins, meanwhile, had needed Gerry Meehan's late-game goal against Philadelphia in Buffalo's regular-season finale to simply get into the postseason. So it was entirely predictable that Chicago would win the first three games of the series, which the Blackhawks did. What few anticipated, though, was that the Penguins would battle them so fiercely, and that didn't change when the Penguins were facing elimination in Game 4. They built a 4–2 lead over the first 40 minutes, then forced overtime with a Bobby Leiter goal at 17:52 of the third period. The Penguins entered overtime knowing that they would send the best-of-seven back to Chicago Stadium if they could manufacture a sixth goal on Blackhawks goalie Gerry Desjardins. Twelve seconds later, their season was over. Chicago center Pit Martin controlled a face-off against Leiter at center ice and sent the puck into the Penguins' end, and Penguins goalie Jim Rutherford left his crease to get it. "I thought I had my glove on it," he said. "But I'm really not sure if I did." Martin said Rutherford did, but that Chicago forward Jim Pappin knocked it loose, toward Eddie Shack of the Penguins. Martin charged at Shack and knocked the puck away from him. In a heartbeat, the puck went off the skate of Penguins defenseman Tim Horton and into the net. "It wasn't very complicated," Horton said. "The puck hit my skate and went in." Martin got credit for the goal. The Penguins got started on their offseason.

Hall of Fame defenseman Tim Horton's one-year stay in Pittsburgh came to an abrupt and unfortunate end.
© PITTSBURGH PENGUINS

NOVEMBER 22, 1972

THAT WAS QUICK

ST. LOUIS was the West Division's dominant team and the Penguins' biggest rival for a number of years after both entered the NHL in 1967, which might help to explain why the Blues were involved in so many of the major memories from the Penguins' early seasons. One of the biggest—and perhaps most surprising, since it didn't involve anyone throwing punches—occurred during the third period of what had been, to that point, a relatively uneventful game at the Civic Arena. The teams were tied 3–3 at the second intermission. Fran Huck beat Jim Rutherford at 1:22 of the third, but Syl Apps countered for the Penguins just 34 seconds later. Things proceeded without so much as a minor penalty until the middle of the period approached, when Greg Polis put the Penguins up, 5–4. And then it happened, like it never happened before or since in NHL history, as the Penguins scored five goals in two minutes and seven seconds to transform what had been a tight game into a 10–4 victory. Bryan Hextall, Jean Pronovost, Al McDonough, Ken Schinkel, and Ron Schock were responsible for the third-period onslaught against Blues goalie Wayne Stephenson. The rampage began with eight minutes remaining in regulation and ended 127 seconds later, with the Penguins needing just 27 seconds to get their final three goals. Among the individual feats that stood out in this game: Apps had a goal and three assists, and McDonough recorded his third hat trick of 1972–73.

Right winger Jean Pronovost was one of the Penguins' most prolific goal-scorers during the franchise's early years.
COURTESY OF GETTY IMAGES

JANUARY 30, 1973

HEADY TIMES FOR GREG POLIS

EARNING AN invitation to an NHL All-Star Game—let alone being recognized as the outstanding player in it—would be a career highlight for a lot of guys. For Penguins winger Greg Polis, it wasn't even the most memorable thing that happened to him that week. That's because Polis, making his third all-star appearance, had become a first-time father little more than 24 hours before scoring two goals in the game at Madison Square Garden. "I looked at my baby [a son, Jason] for the first time 20 minutes after he was born," Polis said. "He wasn't washed yet and I said to myself, 'What a miracle.' I thought I'd try to play well for my child in the All-Star Game so that someday I could tell him about it. I thought if I was able to score a goal, I'd save the puck for him when he grows up." Well, Polis was able to get two of those for his boy, and a car, too, if he was inclined to part with it at some point in the distant future. Polis opened the scoring 55 seconds into the second period, when he rapped a Bobby Clarke rebound past East goalie Gilles Villemure. He picked up his second early in the third period, trimming the East squad's lead over Polis's West team to 5–4. Los Angeles defenseman Terry Harper would pull the West even at 9:27, but at 13:59 the East moved in front to stay when Bobby Schmautz of Vancouver (yes, Vancouver was in the East) put a shot behind Ed Giacomin. So Polis's club lost, but he left New York very much a winner.

Left winger Greg Polis was a reliable offensive producer for the Penguins. COURTESY OF GETTY IMAGES

The tag team of Bob Kelly and Steve Durbano was an instant hit after being acquired from St. Louis.
© PITTSBURGH PENGUINS

JANUARY 16, 1974

"DEMOLITION" DURBANO, "BATTLESHIP" KELLY ARRIVE

WHILE THE Penguins' rivalry with St. Louis also was ferocious in the early years following the 1967 expansion, it often was rather one-sided, as the Blues generally had a decided edge in size and overall nastiness. Penguins GM Jack Button decided to address that by sending high-scoring winger Greg Polis and rugged defenseman Bryan Watson to the Blues for skilled defenseman Ab DeMarco and two heavyweights—left winger Bob (Battleship) Kelly and defenseman Steve (Demolition Durby) Durbano. Blues president Sid Salomon III said he worked out the deal with Penguins owner Tad Potter, although the Penguins insisted it was Button's first major move after replacing Jack Riley as GM. Salomon said he initiated talks with Potter because he felt it was necessary to acquire Polis after St. Louis had lost four games in a row. The Penguins proposed getting DeMarco and Durbano for him, with Watson and Kelly added to the mix when Pittsburgh decided it needed a left winger to replace Polis. The finer points of the negotiations aside, Durbano and Kelly gave the Penguins a major infusion of toughness. That was evident during a 4–1 win over the Blues a week after the trade, when Kelly fought Bob Plager and Durbano traded punches with Bob Gassoff. "The Blues won't be bothering us too much anymore," Kelly said. "I don't think anyone will bother us too much."

Syl Apps became the second Penguins played to be named MVP of an NHL All-Star Game.
COURTESY OF GETTY IMAGES

JANUARY 21, 1975

A FAMILY AFFAIR FOR APPS

SYL APPS didn't expect to win a car when he was selected to play in an NHL All-Star Game for the first time. Frankly, what he had in mind was far more modest. "I was afraid to make a mistake in front of all the best hockey players," he said. "I didn't want to be embarrassed in front of all those people on television and my family." That family included his father, Hockey Hall of Famer Syl Apps Sr. And if Apps the Younger did anything wrong, it seemed to pass unnoticed after he scored two goals to lead the Wales Conference past the Campbell Conference 7–1 at the Forum in Montreal. "I've had a lot of thrills in hockey, but this is one of the best," Apps Sr. said. Apps Jr., who scored his team's first and fifth goals, acknowledged that he hadn't gone to the game anticipating that he could have a major impact. "I was just happy to be here," he said. His father was thrilled as well, but allowed that he was hoping his son would make it onto the score sheet at least one more time. "I kept hoping for that third goal," Apps Sr. said. "He almost got it three times." Although Apps wasn't expecting to return to Pittsburgh with a new car, the one he earned in Montreal came along at an ideal time. "We need two cars," he said. "And the lease on the one the team gave me expires in 10 days."

Coach Marc Boileau led the Penguins to a franchise-record unbeaten streak on home ice.
© PITTSBURGH PENGUINS

FEBRUARY 22, 1975

THERE'S NO PLACE LIKE HOME

PENGUINS COACH Marc Boileau was a realist after the Penguins' 3–2 decision over St. Louis at the Civic Arena, a victory that stretched their unbeaten streak on home ice to 12–0–8. He acknowledged the day would come when his team would be beaten there. Boileau just didn't see much reason to think it would happen anytime soon. "Sure, this is going to end," he said. "Sometime in June or July." Turned out that it only held up for another 24 hours, because Detroit beat the Penguins 3–1, thanks largely to a 36-save effort by Red Wings goalie Jim Rutherford. Nonetheless, going 20 in a row at home without losing was a remarkable feat, something only four clubs had managed to that point in league history. The Penguins had seemed well on their way to beating the Blues when Lowell MacDonald scored his second of the game at 6:32 of the third period to put them up, 3–0, but Bill Collins and Doug Palazzari of St. Louis beat Penguins goalie Michel Plasse in a span of 76 seconds midway through the period to inject some serious suspense into the outcome.

MARCH 8, 1975

STACKING UP ASSISTS

DEFENSEMAN RON STACKHOUSE, one of the most polarizing figures in franchise history, became the first Pittsburgh player to record six assists in a game when he managed the feat in an 8–2 win over Philadelphia on home ice. It was an achievement no Penguins defenseman would match until Kris Letang did it December 27, 2023, on Long Island. The six-assist games by those two defensemen bookended four by Pittsburgh forwards—the first by Greg Malone, the other three by Mario Lemieux. Although he was six foot three, 210 pounds, Stackhouse's style was based on finesse, not physicality, and that made him the target of frequent verbal abuse from a segment of the Pittsburgh fan base. It was not the least bit unusual to hear some leather-lunged fan, generally in the upper reaches of the Civic Arena, bellow, "Hit him with your purse, Stackhouse," after he passed on an opportunity to deliver a body check. Against the Flyers, most of Stackhouse's passing went to teammates, and often resulted in a goal. His productivity tied a single-game record for NHL defensemen, and in the process he became the 13th player in the league to record four assists in a period as Pittsburgh outscored the Flyers 5–0 during the second. The sellout crowd of 13,404—well, most of it, anyway—might not have recognized the magnitude of what Stackhouse did over the course of those 60 minutes, but it appreciated seeing archrival Philadelphia humbled in such a lopsided defeat.

Ron Stackhouse played a game that was long on finesse, short on physicality.
COURTESY OF GETTY IMAGES

Center Pierre Larouche was a fixture on the exciting Penguins teams of the mid-1970s.
COURTESY OF GETTY IMAGES

MARCH 15, 1975

CAPITALS PUNISHMENT

EXPANSION TEAMS generally struggle during the first season or two in existence, but Washington took that concept to new lows when it entered the NHL in 1974–75. The Capitals finished with an 8–67–5 record and, at one point, lost 37 consecutive games on the road. There were, obviously, a lot of lows for Washington during that inaugural season, but the Penguins drove the Capitals to depths rarely reached by beating them 12–1 at the Civic Arena. Pierre Larouche, Vic Hadfield, and Rick Kehoe had two goals each for the Penguins, who also got single goals from forwards Syl Apps, Lowell MacDonald, Bob Kelly, Lew Morrison, and Bob McManama and defenseman Barry Wilkins. By the time the game was over, no fewer than 15 Pittsburgh players, including goalie Gary Inness, had collected at least one point. Defenseman Yvan Labre, a Penguins alum, was the only Washington player to get a puck past Inness. "We were moving the puck all night," Pittsburgh coach Marc Boileau said. "It was like a pinball machine out there." When the Penguins weren't moving pucks, they were depositing them behind Capitals goalies Michel Belhumeur and Ron Low.

APRIL 26, 1975

THE BITTER END

THE PENGUINS had a joyride through most of the 1974–75 season, including a sweep of St. Louis in a best-of-three series during the opening round of the Stanley Cup playoffs. But after winning the first three games of the next round against the New York Islanders, Pittsburgh gained a place in league history that no club ever would want: It lost the next four in a row, becoming only the second club in league history to be defeated in a best-of-seven series after capturing the first three games. "We were overconfident, definitely," Penguins coach Marc Boileau said. New York's rebound was keyed by backup goalie Glenn (Chico) Resch, who replaced Billy Smith in the Islanders' net after the Penguins moved to within one victory of a matchup with Philadelphia in the next round. But New York needed some Game 7 heroics by Ed Westfall at the Civic Arena to complete the comeback. He scored the only goal of the game with 5:18 remaining in regulation, beating Pittsburgh goalie Gary Inness with a rising backhander. While Westfall's goal sealed their fate, the Penguins were convinced the series got away from them when they squandered their first chance to close out the Islanders, dropping a 3–1 decision at Nassau Coliseum in Game 4. "That was the turning point," captain Ron Schock said. "We let them off the hook."

Islanders forward Ed Westfall, being checked by Ron Schock, scored the goal that secured New York's historic comeback. COURTESY OF GETTY IMAGES

GM Jack Button, flanked by part-owners Peter Block and Tad Potter, discuss the team's financial plight. COURTESY OF GETTY IMAGES

JUNE 13, 1975

THE IRS COMES CALLING

THEIR HISTORIC collapse against the New York Islanders in Round 2 of the playoffs wasn't the Penguins' most significant setback in the first half of 1975. In mid-June the team offices were padlocked by the Internal Revenue Service and the Penguins promptly filed for bankruptcy, a move designed to prevent the franchise's creditors from seizing control of its assets—the players. The IRS claimed that the Penguins, who were the first NHL team to file for bankruptcy since before World War II, owed it more than a half million dollars in the form of tax that was withheld from the players but not turned over to the government. In addition to their issues with the IRS, the Penguins owed $5 million in loans to Equibank and $1 million to the NHL. GM Jack Button, who had overseen the Penguins' rise from near-comical to competitive, was named receiver and given until September 30 to draw up a reorganization plan to pay those debts. Despite facing what he called an "awesome burden," Button tried to maintain an upbeat perspective on the franchise's long-term future. "I remain confident the Penguins will prosper and survive and will remain in Pittsburgh," he said.

MARCH 24, 1976

PRONOVOST, LAROUCHE MAKE THEIR MARKS

JEAN PRONOVOST joined an elite club when he scored his 50th goal of the season, and he said his accomplishment was "a wonderful feeling, hard to describe." He would have been a lot happier, though, if his third-period goal, which gave the Penguins a 4–3 lead over Boston at the Civic Arena, had proved to be the difference-maker in what ended as a 5–5 tie. "It would have been much better," he said, "if my goal would have stood up as the winning goal." Pronovost did get a bit of consolation, though, by assisting on linemate Syl Apps's goal with 48 seconds remaining in regulation to salvage a point against the Bruins. Pronovost's milestone largely overshadowed one attained by second-year center Pierre Larouche, whose 45th goal of the season at 17:09 of the first period doubled as his 100th point, allowing him to supplant Bobby Orr as the youngest player to hit triple digits in a season. It was a momentous achievement, although Larouche, 20, insisted that he didn't know why anyone would focus on it, given what Pronovost had done. "Getting 100 points is nothing to be excited about," he said. "[Pronovost] getting his 50th goal is the big thing tonight. Getting 50 goals is a hockey player's dream, and 100 points doesn't compare to that." Maybe not, but Larouche's teammates were impressed by what he had done. "Right from the start, you knew Pierre had the talent," Vic Hadfield said. "Players like him don't come along too often."

Pierre Larouche, a skilled and creative center, often was a step ahead of most Penguins opponents. COURTESY OF GETTY IMAGES

Goalie Michel Plasse couldn't prevent St. Louis from rallying after Jean Pronovost got the Penguins off to a record-tying start.
© PITTSBURGH PENGUINS

MARCH 25, 1976

STARTING FAST

JEAN PRONOVOST, fresh off getting his 50th goal of the season the previous evening, needed just six seconds to stake the Penguins to a 1–0 lead over the archrival Blues at St. Louis Arena. The goal, which tied the league record held by Henry Boucha of Detroit, remains the team's fastest goal after a game-opening face-off. Unfortunately for the Penguins, they were able to get only one more puck past Blues goalie Ed Staniowski, while St. Louis deposited four behind Michel Plasse before he gave way to Bobby Taylor in what became a 5–2 victory for the home team. Staniowski finished with 33 saves and was the dominant presence in the game. That was quite different than his previous start against Pittsburgh 12 days earlier, when he had been a 7–1 loser at the Civic Arena. "I think I played just as well the last time," Staniowski said. "The team just played that much better in front of me." The final score—and a concussion that caused Vic Hadfield to spend the night in a hospital after he hit his head on the ice following a check by Blues defenseman Barclay Plager—aside, there were a few positives for the Penguins in this game. Syl Apps's assist on Pronovost's goal was his 63rd of the season, tying a team record, and Pierre Larouche extended his scoring streak to 11 games.

APRIL 14, 1979

FERGUSON DULLS THE SABRES

THERE WERE precious few highlights for the Penguins as the 1970s were winding down, but George Ferguson provided one with his goal 47 seconds into overtime of a 4–3 victory in Game 3 of the Penguins' opening-round series against Buffalo, securing their upset of the Sabres and a place in the second round of the playoffs. Ferguson, whose third-period goal had tied the game, 3–3, took a feed from center Gregg Sheppard and carried the puck into the Buffalo end before lashing a shot past Sabres goalie Bob Sauve for the series-winner. "I noticed the left side of the rink was open," Ferguson said. "So I just took off, and when I thought I could score, I just let it fly. I don't think it was anything different than I've been doing all season. But it sure meant a whole lot more." The Penguins actually were fortunate to make it past the third period, considering that Ferguson got the only goal for either team, even though Buffalo enjoyed an 18–3 advantage in shots then. "I figured when we forced them into overtime after they had the kind of period they had just had, we had a good shot at it," Pittsburgh coach Johnny Wilson said. "It has to be a little demoralizing to have that many shots and still not score."

George Ferguson, a speedy winger, was known as "The Fergy Flyer" during his time with the Penguins.
COURTESY OF GETTY IMAGES

Randy Carlyle is the only Penguin to win a Norris Trophy as the NHL's top defenseman. COURTESY OF GETTY IMAGES

JUNE 4, 1981

TROPHY TIME FOR CARLYLE, KEHOE

RANDY CARLYLE was awarded the Penguins' only Norris Trophy, which is given annually to the NHL's top defenseman, since the franchise entered the league in the 1967 expansion. He finished the 1980–81 season as the Penguins' number two scorer, with 16 goals and 67 assists in 76 games. Carlyle capped his exceptional season by scoring four goals in five games in the Penguins' opening-round playoff loss to St. Louis, a win the heavily favored Blues were unable to secure until Mike Crombeen scored in double overtime in the finale of the best-of-five series. (Crombeen scored on St. Louis's only shot of the second overtime, while Blues goalie Mike Liut stopped all five the Penguins threw at him then.) Carlyle's closest competition in the Norris balloting came from Denis Potvin of the New York Islanders and Montreal's Larry Robinson. Carlyle ended up with 120 votes, while Potvin, who had won the trophy three times in the previous five years, received 113 and Robinson, who got the Norris the two times Potvin did not, had 100. On the same day Carlyle received his Norris, high-scoring right winger Rick Kehoe was given the Lady Byng Trophy, which recognizes sportsmanship and productive play. Kehoe, who had finished the regular season with five more points than Carlyle while being assessed a total of just three minor penalties, edged runner-up Wayne Gretzky in the Byng voting, 138–120. Carlyle and Kehoe, like that year's other trophy winners, were awarded $1,500 by the league.

FEBRUARY 21, 1982

DION, BULLARD STYMIE THE ISLANDERS

THE PENGUINS and New York Islanders have had an intriguing history. New York has wrecked Pittsburgh's playoff hopes several times over the years, and the Penguins have hit some improbable high points while facing Islanders clubs that had dramatically superior personnel. And so it was that the Penguins, especially with their lineup ravaged by injuries to key players, were an unlikely candidate to end the Islanders' league-record 15-game winning streak, but that's just what they did with a 4–3 victory at the Civic Arena. The Penguins had been sputtering going into weekend games against Philadelphia and the Islanders, but came away with one-goal victories in both—which was something not even coach Eddie Johnston had anticipated. "If anybody told me, the way we were going, that we'd have a weekend like this, I'd have bet my house," he said, laughing. "We were coming off a big win [against the Flyers] and we didn't want to fall on our faces. We got 110 percent from everybody tonight because we knew playing 90 percent against a team like the Islanders wasn't going to do it for us." Mike Bullard was the offensive hero for the Penguins, scoring two goals in the third period. The first tied the score, and the second was the game winner. But even Bullard's contribution to the victory was overshadowed by that of goalie Michel Dion, who was named the game's number one star after stopping 32 of 35 shots to earn the victory, his first in nine lifetime appearances against the Islanders. "I really wanted to beat them, because I had never beaten them before," Dion said. "They were giving me indigestion."

Center Mike Bullard showed that he could score goals in bunches.
COURTESY OF GETTY IMAGES

APRIL 13, 1982

OH, SO CLOSE ON LONG ISLAND

THE NEW YORK Islanders entered their best-of-five playoff series against the Penguins as two-time defending Stanley Cup champions, and after dominating Games 1 and 2 by scores of 8–1 and 7–2, respectively, the only uncertainty—and there was just a tiny sliver of it—was whether the Islanders would complete the sweep. But the Penguins, against all odds and logic, rallied to win Games 3 and 4 at the Civic Arena and send the series back to Nassau Coliseum for a series-deciding showdown. And with less than six minutes to go in the third period of Game 5, the Penguins were on the cusp of one of the biggest upsets in playoff history, holding a 3–1 lead. "I was feeling really high," coach Eddie Johnston said. But then Mike McEwen got the Islanders within one by scoring on a power play at 14:33, and New York pulled even on a John Tonelli goal at 17:39. That put the game into a winner-take-all overtime, and Tonelli made sure New York took it all by beating Penguins goalie Michel Dion with the last of his team's 46 shots. Tonelli's series winner came after Islanders goalie Billy Smith had made a sensational save on Penguins center Mike Bullard. Had Bullard's shot eluded Smith, Pittsburgh would have moved on to a semifinal matchup with Philadelphia. Instead, it was New York that advanced to meet the Flyers. "We're pleased and relieved," Islanders right winger Bobby Nystrom said. "And thanking our lucky stars."

Goalie Michel Dion almost made it possible for the Penguins to pull off one of the greatest upsets in playoff history.
COURTESY OF GETTY IMAGES

MARCH 15, 1983

ANOTHER DOSE OF TRAGEDY

PENGUINS GENERAL manager Aldege "Baz" Bastien was killed in an accident on the Parkway West in the early-morning hours, when the car he was driving collided with a motorcycle. Coroner Joshua Perper said that Bastien died of a heart attack and head injuries and that a toxicology report showed his blood alcohol level to be .27, nearly three times the limit at which a person was considered to be intoxicated in Pennsylvania. The accident occurred while Bastien was driving home from an event sponsored by the Pittsburgh chapter of the Professional Hockey Writers Association to honor Penguins center Greg Malone. Penguins vice president Paul Martha said that Bastien's death "comes as a complete surprise" and that it was an "unexpected tragedy" and a "big loss for the entire Penguins organization." Bastien, a former goalie, had lost an eye when he was struck by a puck, and disliked driving at night because of his vision issues. That, coupled with the alcohol he had consumed, prompted a number of people at the dinner to prod him to ask someone for a ride home, which many of them believed had been arranged, only to have Bastien leave the gathering without being noticed. Ironically, Bastien died just hours after beginning to reconcile his relationship with coach Eddie Johnston, with whom he had agreed on very little during their time together. "This was the most positive thing we had together in three years," Johnston said. "We cleared the air."

Baz Bastien's tenure as GM ended when he was in a fatal traffic accident.
© PITTSBURGH PENGUINS

Left winger Kevin Stevens developed into an elite power forward with the Penguins. COURTESY OF GETTY IMAGES

SEPTEMBER 9, 1983

A LOW-PROFILE, HIGH-IMPACT TRADE

GM EDDIE JOHNSTON, just a few months into the job he had inherited when Baz Bastien was killed in an auto accident, pulled off one of the most important trades in franchise history—and it went almost unnoticed. He acquired the rights to a left winger named Kevin Stevens, who had been a sixth-round draft choice by Los Angeles that summer, for Anders Hakansson, a capable but unspectacular forward. Stevens would complete four years at Boston College before turning pro, and he spent the better part of the 1988–89 season with the Muskegon Lumberjacks in the International Hockey League. But Stevens would score 40 goals with Pittsburgh during the 1990–91 season and add 17 more during their drive to the team's first championship. His big personality—perhaps the biggest in a locker room that was full of them—helped establish him as an invaluable team leader, and he followed up that 40-goal season by scoring 54, 55, and 41 in the three seasons that followed. Rick Tocchet, who came to know Stevens as an opponent and a teammate, offered this assessment: "When you think of the best power forwards over the years, when you've got a guy like that, plays the game tough, scores 50 goals, great hands, scores clutch in the playoffs, scored some big goals for the Penguins in his career . . . when you talk about that era, the top power forwards, he's in the top."

MARCH 6, 1984

THE DEVILS MADE THEM DO IT

THE ONLY thing the Penguins were competing for as the 1983–84 season was winding down was their place in the order of selection for the NHL Draft. The race to the bottom—which would come with the right to claim superstar-in-waiting Mario Lemieux—was down to two clubs, the Penguins and New Jersey. And while the Devils were adamant that they were trying to win as often as possible, team president Bob Butera suggested the Penguins were doing the opposite. As the Devils were preparing to host the Penguins in a critical game, Butera, a former Pennsylvania legislator, hinted that the Penguins were underachieving by design. "We're trying to win every game, and I hope Pittsburgh is, too," he said. "I'm not being accusatory, but I think Pittsburgh's talent is better than they're showing." That latter point could be debated—those Penguins were a seriously bad team—but there was ample reason to suspect Pittsburgh was intent on finishing last. Nonetheless, after New Jersey's 6-5 victory in the Meadowlands that moved the Devils four points ahead of his team, Penguins coach Lou Angotti lashed back at Butera, in what *The Pittsburgh Press* described as Angotti "peppering his outburst with expletives and numerous vivid, scatological references to Butera." A sampling: "He's got no class. This is a real disgrace. . . . What did we ever do to him?"

Lou Angotti coached the Penguins when they bottomed out during the 1983-84 season.
© PITTSBURGH PENGUINS

JUNE 9, 1984

THE FRANCHISE'S SAVIOR ARRIVES

THE PENGUINS got their payoff for all the bad hockey they committed during the 1983–84 season when they claimed Mario Lemieux with the first selection in the NHL Draft at the Forum in Lemieux's hometown of Montreal. General manager Eddie Johnston, who'd made some late-season moves that seemed designed to hold down his team's point total, never wavered from his plan to add Lemieux, even though that meant turning down numerous trade offers from around the league, They ranged from Quebec suggesting a deal that would have sent the Stastny brothers—Peter, Marian, and Anton—to Pittsburgh, to Minnesota GM Lou Nanne's proposal to send all of the North Stars' selections in that draft to the Penguins for the right to pick Lemieux. While Pittsburgh taking Lemieux was a given, it wasn't clear on draft day when, or even whether, he would join the team, because his agent, Gus Badali, and Johnston were struggling to agree on a contract. The talks were going poorly enough that Lemieux broke with tradition and did not go to the Penguins' team table after they chose him. "I didn't go to the table because negotiations are not going well," he said. "I'm not going to put on the sweater if they don't want me bad enough." The Penguins wanted him very badly, of course, and Johnston and Badali got things worked out just a week later.

The Penguins expected great things from Mario Lemieux when they drafted him in 1984.
COURTESY OF GETTY IMAGES

OCTOBER 11, 1984

THE LEMIEUX DEBUT

O **A LOT** of people were confident that Mario Lemieux would do great things over the course of his career. Not many, though, figured they would start the first time he stepped onto the ice in a National Hockey League game. Wrong. And it would not be anywhere near the last time Lemieux would pull off the nearly unthinkable. Just 78 seconds into his first pro shift, Lemieux stole the puck from Boston all-star defenseman Raymond Bourque in the Penguins' zone, then charged down the ice before throwing a series of dekes at Bruins goalie Pete Peeters and depositing the puck behind him at 2:59 of the opening period. First shift, first shot, first goal. And an excellent first impression. "I'm saying to myself, 'When this guy gets it going, he'll be awesome,' " Peeters said. "He's going to flower after 30, 35 games, after he feels his way around the league." Actually, it was closer to 30 or 35 seconds into Lemieux's first shift when the initial blossoms appeared, since Bourque, still relatively early in his Hall of Fame career, didn't make a habit of losing pucks to opponents. "I tried to pass the puck between his stick and his skate," Bourque said. "It hit his skate and he was just gone. I think he's going to be a big help to that club." Lemieux wasn't quite enough to help the Penguins past Boston, though, as the Bruins left Boston Garden with a 4–3 victory.

Mario Lemieux didn't need long to make his presence felt in the NHL.
COURTESY OF GETTY IMAGES

APRIL 7, 1985

LEMIEUX HITS TRIPLE FIGURES

THE 1984–85 season was, for the most part, one to forget for the Penguins, with the obvious exception of it being Mario Lemieux's first year in the NHL. And lest anyone forget just how much of an impact Lemieux had then, he scored the Penguins' second goal in a 7–3 loss at Washington in the regular-season finale to become just the third first-year player in league history to put up 100 points. "It's a big difference between 100 and 99," Lemieux said. "You work all year and you sure don't want to finish at 99." His only regret, Lemieux added, was that he hadn't gotten to 100 the previous night, during a 7–4 loss to the Capitals at the Civic Arena. "I would have loved to get it . . . in front of our fans," he said. "They've been good to us all year." Hitting that milestone put an exclamation point on a season that made Lemieux the obvious choice to receive the Calder Trophy, which goes annually to the top rookie in the NHL, even though Pittsburgh did not come close to qualifying for the Stanley Cup playoffs. In that same game against the Capitals, Warren Young, Lemieux's linemate and a journeyman left winger who had scored two goals in 20 NHL games over the previous three seasons, racked up number 40 of 1984–85.

Mario Lemieux put a triple-digit exclamation point on his first season as a pro.
COURTESY OF GETTY IMAGES

NOVEMBER 24, 1987

PENGUINS TAKE A COFFEY BREAK

PENGUINS GM Eddie Johnston had been teammates with Bobby Orr in Boston, so he had firsthand knowledge of how much a world-class defenseman can do to help a team. So when Edmonton and Paul Coffey, one of the smoothest-skating, fastest players ever to man his position, were locked in a nasty contract dispute that led to Coffey sitting out the early weeks of the season, he inquired about Coffey's availability and the Oilers' asking price if they were willing to trade him. Edmonton was, and Johnston didn't flinch, acquiring Coffey, along with forwards Dave Hunter and Wayne Van Dorp in exchange for forwards Craig Simpson and Dave Hannan and defensemen Moe Mantha and Chris Joseph. "If you're not interested in Paul Coffey, you've got to be out of your mind," Johnston said. The most obvious beneficiary of having Coffey on his team was Mario Lemieux, because of the way Coffey's talents could mesh with his own. "It's going to be tougher for any team to check me now," Lemieux said. "Coffey comes up on the play all the time, and he can go end-to-end with the puck." The contract issues that had sidelined him in Edmonton were a nonissue with the Penguins. He agreed to play the rest of the season under his existing contract, but got about a 25 percent raise because he would be paid in US, not Canadian, dollars, and he accepted an extension including salaries that went from $400,000 to more than $500,000.

Defenseman Paul Coffey added a volatile dimension to the Penguins' offense after being acquired from Edmonton.
COURTESY OF GETTY IMAGES

Mario Lemieux was widely recognized as the NHL's top player just a few years into his career. COURTESY OF GETTY IMAGES

JUNE 8, 1988

MORE HARDWARE FOR MARIO

O**THE MOST** surprising thing about the voting for the Hart Trophy, awarded annually to the NHL's most valuable player, was not that it went to Mario Lemieux in 1988. Nor that he received first-place votes on 54 of the 63 ballots cast by members of the Professional Hockey Writers Association. Rather, it's that one voter didn't mention him at all, which was rather remarkable considering what Lemieux had accomplished while becoming the fourth Hart recipient whose team failed to qualify for the Stanley Cup playoffs. Still, Lemieux expressed surprise that he, not Wayne Gretzky, had been selected for the Hart, even though Gretzky finished behind teammate Grant Fuhr and received just two first-place votes. "Wayne won this trophy the last eight years and, from my point of view, he's still the best player in the world." While that was magnanimous of Lemieux, it wasn't a widely held opinion. "Right now, [Lemieux] is the best hockey player in the world," said Detroit's Jacques Demers, who was honored as the league's Coach of the Year. "He is the most talented and the most gifted." While he was picking up the Hart at the NHL's awards ceremony in Toronto, Lemieux also got the Art Ross Trophy as the league's leading scorer, making him the first Pittsburgh player to receive either award. The real payoff for Lemieux's work was still to come, however, as the Penguins were preparing to renegotiate his contract.

OCTOBER 7, 1988

COFFEY LIGHTS IT UP

PAUL COFFEY lashed a slap shot past Washington goalie Clint Malarchuk to give the Penguins an insurance goal in what became a 6–4 victory at the Capital Centre in Landover, Maryland. No one realized it at the time, of course, but that goal also was the first of the team-record 30 Coffey would put up in 1988–89. Although he would never come particularly close to matching the personal best of 48 that he scored for Edmonton in 1985–86, Coffey, who was traded to Los Angeles in 1992, still owns the three highest single-season goal totals put up by a Penguins defenseman: 30, 29 (1989–90), and 24 (1990–91). By the time he went to the Kings, Coffey had generated 108 goals and 332 assists in 331 games, more than delivering the impact management was hoping his exceptional skating and skill would have on the team's offense when he was acquired from the Oilers. "A player of Paul Coffey's caliber comes along every 15, 20 years," said Eddie Johnston, the GM who negotiated the deal to add Coffey. "We're looking at a world-class player. They put him in the category of [Bobby] Orr. There's not too many guys like that who come around."

Paul Coffey's offensive game continued to percolate after he joined the Penguins. COURTESY OF GETTY IMAGES

Tom Barrasso filled the Penguins' need for a top-shelf goaltender. COURTESY OF GETTY IMAGES

NOVEMBER 12, 1988

ESPOSITO BRINGS IN BARRASSO

TONY ESPOSITO, then in his early months as general manager of the Penguins, had been a Hall of Fame goaltender during his playing days, so despite any other managerial shortcomings he had, he was fully aware that a quality goalie was a key component of any club that hoped to contend for a championship. With that in mind, Esposito gave Buffalo defenseman Doug Bodger and winger Darrin Shannon, whom Pittsburgh had selected with its first-round pick in the NHL Entry Draft a few months earlier, in return for goalie Tom Barrasso and a third-round draft choice in 1990 that ultimately would be used to claim winger Joe Dziedzic. Barrasso had won both the Vezina Trophy as the NHL's top goaltender and the Calder, as its best rookie, in 1983–84, but had been struggling and was supplanted by Daren Puppa as Buffalo's go-to goalie. "He had a rough start this year," Esposito said. "Didn't play up to his potential." By the time he joined the Penguins, Barrasso's reputation for having strained relationships with some who worked alongside—or had to deal professionally with—him was well-established, but Esposito concluded that adding a goalie of his caliber outweighed any negatives. Negatives, it should be noted, that Barrasso suggested were overstated, if they existed at all. "When I first started, I got a lot of criticism for the way I was," he said. "I've worked pretty hard to change the image I portray to my teammates and in the community."

Mario Lemieux remains the only NHL player ever to pull off the feat he managed against New Jersey. COURTESY OF GETTY IMAGES

DECEMBER 31, 1988

FIVE GOALS, FIVE WAYS

MARIO LEMIEUX didn't retire as the only player to win more than one Stanley Cup. Far from it, obviously. And there were others who collected multiple scoring titles and MVP awards, too. But Lemieux was—and remains—the only guy to get all five possible types of goals in an NHL game. He did it in an 8-6 victory over New Jersey at the Civic Arena. He scored at even strength, on the power play, while Pittsburgh was shorthanded, on a penalty shot, and into an empty net. And while it's not entirely clear whether the latter actually crossed the goal line before time expired—"I don't know whether it was a good goal or not," Lemieux said—the goal stood and Lemieux had an entry in the league record book all to himself. "I think it was just another average night for him," said Lemieux's right winger, Rob Brown. "He just decided this was going to be his game, and nobody else's. Some of the things he did out there were amazing. . . . Even when he wasn't scoring goals, he was putting the puck through his legs, making twirls . . . it was a classic example of the best hockey player in the world teaching us how to play." Two of Lemieux's goals actually were scored while the Penguins were shorthanded, because he converted his penalty shot against New Jersey goalie Chris Terreri while the Penguins were killing a hooking minor to Dan Quinn.

FEBRUARY 2, 1989

AT LONG LAST, IT'S OVER

SOME BAD streaks in sports feel as if they might last forever. This one almost did. When the Penguins walked into the Spectrum to face the Flyers, they did it knowing that 15 years and 42 games has passed since the last time they left Philadelphia with two points, way back on January 20, 1974. Fact is, they had earned a total of just three points during that decade and a half, going 0–39–3 and usually not looking very good in the process. But at 10:34 p.m., the Penguins' 5–3 victory was official and they were free of the Nightmare on Broad Street that had been a burden for the franchise for so long. "I'm going to savor it," forward Dave Hannan said. "Because I've had my head between my legs leaving here many times after getting beat." The winning goalie, Wendell Young, had spent a lot of nights in the Spectrum, too, since he was a former Flyer. But he didn't do his ex-teammates any favors, stopping 36 of their 39 shots. "It's more satisfying coming back and breaking the streak," Young said. "It's just a little bit extra added to it that I was facing my old teammates." Frankly, the Penguins didn't care what motivated him. All that mattered was ending the streak. "We had to do something about it," coach Gene Ubriaco said. "It was getting a little ridiculous."

Ex-Flyers goalie Wendell Young helped to end the Penguins' 42-game winless streak in Philadelphia.
COURTESY OF GETTY IMAGES

APRIL 25, 1989

ALTHOUGH MARIO LEMIEUX did some remarkable things during his early years in the NHL, he didn't make the playoffs until the end of his fifth season. Once he finally made it, he clearly intended to make his mark, and he did that in a big way in Game 5 of the Penguins' second-round series against Philadelphia. Lemieux had five goals and three assists in a 10–7 victory at the Civic Arena that lifted the Penguins to a 3–2 edge in the best-of-seven. "We ran into a tremendous snowball with No. 66 on it," Flyers coach Paul Holmgren said. "And when that gets rolling at you, it's tough to stop." Even Lemieux was willing to admit that, yeah, his work in Game 5 wasn't very shabby. "I've had a lot of great games," he said. "But under pressure like that—a key game for the team—I think that was one of the best." Not just one of his personal best. One of the best individual showings in a game since clubs began competing for the Stanley Cup. Lemieux's eight points tied the NHL playoff record set by New Jersey's Patrik Sundstrom in 1988, and his five goals matched the league mark set by Newsy Lalonde in 1919 and matched by Maurice Richard, Darryl Sittler, and Reggie Leach. Lemieux's four goals in the first period also tied the single-period record set by Tim Kerr of Philadelphia four years earlier. Unfortunately for Lemieux and the Penguins, their playoff run ended two games later.

Mario Lemieux could make an eight-point game look almost normal.
COURTESY OF GETTY IMAGES

The Penguins made a franchise-altering move when they hired Craig Patrick as general manager.
COURTESY OF GETTY IMAGES

Craig Patrick
COURTESY OF GETTY IMAGES

DECEMBER 5, 1989

FRONT OFFICE MAKEOVER

THE PENGUINS went into the 1989–90 season as a popular choice to finish first in the Patrick Division, but by early December they were mired in fifth place, with a 10–14–2 record. And while it probably wasn't what influenced their decision on who should replace GM Tony Esposito and coach Gene Ubriaco, the guy who was chosen to fill those roles was the grandson of the guy after whom the division was named. That would be Craig Patrick, whose grandfather was Lester Patrick. "If we were going to do anything, we felt that we had to have a major reorganization," said Paul Martha, the team's vice president. "There was a dissatisfaction with the direction the organization was taking." Edward DeBartolo Jr., son of the team's owner, echoed that sentiment, saying that, "We're not making a change just to make a change. . . . I feel very, very confident that Craig Patrick is the man to run the organization and lead the team." Patrick agreed to serve not only as GM, but as interim coach. He had been a forward in the NHL, an assistant coach with the 1980 US Olympic team, GM of the New York Rangers, and athletic director at his alma mater, the University of Denver. "This is the perfect situation for me and what I want to accomplish," Patrick said. "My immediate goal is success as soon as possible without jeopardizing the future of the Pittsburgh Penguins."

JANUARY 21, 1990

HE'S THE BRIGHTEST STAR . . . AGAIN

MARIO LEMIEUX wasted no time putting his fingerprints all over the first NHL All-Star Game played in Pittsburgh. Lemieux, who previously had earned all-star MVP honors in 1985 (Calgary)—which made him the first rookie in league history to accomplish that feat—and 1988 (St. Louis), scored four goals at the Civic Arena to pick up his third MVP award, more than any player before him. (By that time, Lemieux had won so many cars that he might have been thinking about opening a dealership.) "You could sense that he wanted to perform really well," Boston winger Cam Neely said. "And he certainly did." Lemieux didn't wait long to do it, either. Just 21 seconds after the opening face-off, he threw a backhander past Campbell Conference goalie Mike Vernon. "Right from the first shift, he just took control," said Philadelphia left winger Brian Propp, Lemieux's linemate for the day. By the time the first intermission arrived, Lemieux had scored two more, giving him a firm grip on every part of the MVP car with the possible exception of the rear bumper and perhaps a hubcap. "When I scored early, it took a lot of pressure away," Lemieux said. "Anytime you get a good start, you feel like getting a couple more." Turned out that three wasn't quite enough to satisfy him, so Lemieux added number four after Kirk McLean replaced Vernon in goal. "I got to show a lot of people that I was a good hockey player," Lemieux said.

Mario Lemieux's four-goal rampage delighted the home crowd at the 1990 NHL All-Star Game.
COURTESY OF GETTY IMAGES

Crippling back pain aborted Mario Lemieux's bid for the longest scoring streak in NHL history. COURTESY OF GETTY IMAGES

FEBRUARY 14, 1990

THE STREAK ENDS

FINALLY, AT SOME point in the second period at Madison Square Garden, the pain in his back simply became too great and Mario Lemieux hobbled to the Penguins' locker room. He didn't return before the Penguins' 4–3 overtime victory over the New York Rangers was complete, so when his night's work was over his 46-game point streak ended, too, leaving him five games shy of matching Wayne Gretzky's NHL record. "After the first period, he just said, 'I can't help the team,'" interim coach Craig Patrick said. Outdoing Gretzky had been driving Lemieux, but when his mobility on the ice suffered by comparison to that of a marble statue, he realized that not surrendering to his condition was futile. "It's tough to not get a chance to get out there," Lemieux said. "It's tough to accept, but that's the way it goes." His teammates knew Lemieux had been playing with a herniated disk in his back, but still were disappointed that his streak was over. "It just doesn't seem fair," left winger Troy Loney said. "You hate to see it end because of an injury. If the guy had been able to give it his all tonight, he'd still have that streak going. We all know that." The initial word from Patrick was that Lemieux, who had a league-leading 121 points, "just really needs some rest" and that Patrick had "no idea" when he would resume playing.

MARCH 31, 1990

A NIGHT OF DRAMA AND DEFEAT

THE PENGUINS entered their regular-season finale against Buffalo figuring that they were facing a 60-minute season. They were wrong. It actually lasted 61. And when it ended, after Sabres defenseman Uwe Krupp had beaten Penguins goalie Tom Barrasso with a shot from the left point one minute into overtime, the Penguins' season was over, because they had needed to take two points from Buffalo to finish ahead of the New York Islanders for the final playoff spot in the Patrick Division. (A victory would have pulled the Penguins even with the Islanders, but the Penguins would have won the tiebreaker.) The abrupt and bitter ending spoiled the extraordinary return of Mario Lemieux, who had missed the previous 21 games while undergoing treatments in California for the back problems that torpedoed his bid to break Wayne Gretzky's record of putting up points in 51 consecutive games. Lemieux flew across the country the day before the Buffalo game, and despite not being on the ice since February 14, set up the Penguins' first goal and scored their second in a 3–2 defeat. He tied the game 2–2 early in the third period by driving a 55-foot shot past Buffalo goalie Clint Malarchuk. "I felt good until the third period, when I started to get a little bit tired," Lemieux said. Perhaps, but it really didn't show in his play, which exceeded all reasonable expectations for someone whose involvement in the game probably should have been limited to watching it on TV.

Not even Mario Lemieux's heroics could give the Penguins what they needed to get into the 1990 playoffs.
COURTESY OF GETTY IMAGES

JUNE 12, 1990

"WHY NOT GET THE BEST?"

CRAIG PATRICK had spent about a half year as the Penguins' GM and interim coach when he decided it was time to hire a full-time coach and an experienced personnel man for his front office. And he did it while following a pretty basic philosophy of management: "I've always been taught to surround yourself with great people," Patrick said. "Why not get the best?" By bringing in Bob Johnson as coach and Scotty Bowman as director of player development, Patrick certainly made a compelling case that he'd accomplished what he set out to do. "In my opinion, we have the best management team in hockey," he said. "I think we're going to be a perfect fit, just because I understand what we all want to accomplish. We all have the same goal." For Johnson, one of the game's great optimists, that meant getting back behind the bench after spending three years as executive director at USA Hockey. "I'm a guy who enjoys going to the rink," said Johnson, who had coached Calgary after a long stint at the University of Wisconsin. "I'm very positive, very enthusiastic." While the coaching of Johnson's two immediate full-time predecessors, Gene Ubriaco and Pierre Creamer, was viewed skeptically by many of their players, Johnson's hiring was met with universal approval in the locker room, including by the most important guy there. "There's no doubt in anybody's mind that Bob Johnson has proven himself to be a great coach," Mario Lemieux said.

Craig Patrick gave his management team a bold upgrade by hiring Bob Johnson and Scotty Bowman. COURTESY OF GETTY IMAGES

Jaromir Jagr was a nice consolation prize after four clubs picked ahead of the Penguins in the 1990 NHL Draft.
COURTESY OF GETTY IMAGES

JUNE 16, 1990

CRAIG PATRICK DOES THE RIGHT THING

O **AN NHL** general manager rarely is able to add two future Hall of Famers at the same position on the same day, but that's what Craig Patrick pulled off at the NHL Draft in Vancouver. He acquired two right wingers, Jaromir Jagr and Joe Mullen, who would prove to be major contributors to the Penguins' championships in 1991 and 1992. Patrick chose Jagr with the fifth pick in the draft and got Mullen from Calgary for a second-round pick. Mullen was 33, but he had been named to the NHL all-star team in each of the previous two seasons and had been named one of the league's five most underrated players in a poll of NHL players during the 1989–90 season. Jagr, who was from Czechoslovakia, was in a group expected to be claimed with the first five choices; the others were Owen Nolan, Petr Nedved, Keith Primeau, and Mike Ricci. Being from Eastern Europe is why Jagr slipped to number five because, as Patrick noted, "Dealing with Eastern Bloc countries is not the easiest thing to do," and the other four prospects were highly regarded. Jagr, though, always was atop the Penguins' list because, Patrick said, they "felt all along that he was the most talented player in the draft." Jagr, speaking through a translator, left no doubt that he craved an opportunity to share a line with Mario Lemieux. "I would be overjoyed," he said. "That would be wonderful. But I don't know how Mario Lemieux could stand it."

Craig Patrick filled some key needs when he brought in Ron Francis, Ulf Samuelsson, and Grant Jennings from Hartford. COURTESY OF GETTY IMAGES

MARCH 4, 1991

A WHALE OF A TRADE

O**CRAIG PATRICK** realized, as the NHL trade deadline approached, that his team had the potential to do some great things in the spring. He also recognized that the Penguins had some gaping holes in their lineup that might prevent them from doing so. So Patrick went about negotiating what might be the most important trade any Pittsburgh GM ever made, adding excellent two-way center Ron Francis, rugged defenseman Ulf Samuelsson, and utility man Grant Jennings from Hartford in exchange for high-scoring center John Cullen, gifted defenseman Zarley Zalapski, and forward Jeff Parker. "We lost two people [Cullen and Zalapski] who have contributed an awful lot to our success, especially in the early going this year," Patrick said. "You hate to give up people like that, but when you think about improving your clubs, sometimes you have to part with people you're not excited about losing. Cullen, an outstanding playmaker who was racking up points at an impressive rate, had no interest in leaving the Penguins, but understood the deal from their perspective. "Pittsburgh is getting some great players," he said. Francis, inexplicably, had fallen out of favor with Hartford's ownership and Whalers coach Rick Ley, who, three months earlier, had stripped Francis of the captaincy he had held since February 1985 because he didn't think Francis was "fiery" enough to maintain that position. "I'm not bitter, but I'm disappointed," Francis told the *Hartford Courant* upon learning of the trade. "I was publicly demeaned every day."

The Penguins earned their first-ever division title in 1991 and followed that a few months later by celebrating their first Stanley Cup championship.
COURTESY OF GETTY IMAGES

MARCH 27, 1991

PENGUINS FINALLY EARN A BANNER

IT TOOK the better part of a quarter century, but the Penguins finally won a division championship with a 7–4 victory at Joe Louis Arena in Detroit. "We can finally put up a banner in Pittsburgh," winger Mark Recchi said. "And it's going to be a great feeling when we do." Ironically, Mario Lemieux, who had been singlehandedly responsible for reviving the franchise seven years earlier but was sidelined for much of the season because of a serious back infection, was not in uniform against the Red Wings. In this case, though, his back had nothing to do with it. He had been struck near the left eye by a puck during a game in Philadelphia the previous evening, and it was all but swollen shut when the game in Detroit began. "We played 50 games without him the same way we played tonight," coach Bob

Johnson said. "We gutted it out." With Lemieux out of the personnel mix, the Penguins swamped Detroit with a diversified attack. Rookie Jaromir Jagr scored two goals, while Paul Coffey, Bryan Trottier, Kevin Stevens, Ron Francis, and Scott Young added one each. They also got some pretty good goaltending from Frank Pietrangelo, who hadn't started in a month but made 28 saves en route to his 10th victory of the season.

"I hadn't played in a long time and I was looking forward to it," he said. "Then when I found out it was going to be tonight, I saw an opportunity. I saw, it would be great to be a part of history." And so he was at 10:34 p.m., when the game—and the Penguins' streak of seasons without a title—ended. "This is what it's all about, winning championships," Lemieux said. "There's no better feeling in the world."

Frank Pietrangelo's glove stop on Peter Stastny of New Jersey remains among the most celebrated saves in team history. COURTESY OF GETTY IMAGES

APRIL 13, 1991

THE SAVE OF A LIFETIME

FRANK PIETRANGELO was supposed to spend the evening at the far end of the bench watching Tom Barrasso, the Penguins' franchise goaltender, try to keep their season alive. But Barrasso had injured his right shoulder during Game 5 of Pittsburgh's first-round playoff series against New York, so Pietrangelo was pressed into service. He responded by stopping 28 of the Devils' 31 shots, including one that will forever be remembered in team annals as "The Save." The Penguins were leading 2–1 late in the first period when New Jersey center Peter Stastny had the puck alone in front of the Penguins' net. When Stastny threw it toward Pietrangelo, the crowd at Brendan Byrne Arena celebrated. Until Pietrangelo tossed the puck out of his glove, anyway. It was a moment that will live forever in franchise history, even though Pietrangelo was quick to acknowledged that all of his work and training and talent had nothing to do with denying Stastny. "It's just instinct for a goalie to reach back and put anything he can in there," Pietrangelo said. "He hit my glove. It's not a matter of a skill save; it's a lucky save." That good fortune played the leading role in that stop is undeniable—what were the chances that Stastny, who scored 450 times in 977 career games, would shoot into the exact space filled by Pietrangelo's glove?—but even Pietrangelo acknowledged that "when you make a save like that, lucky or not, it's a big lift for the team."

Kevin Stevens could be as much of a force in the locker room as he was on the ice. COURTESY OF GETTY IMAGES

MAY 3, 1991

KEVIN STEVENS TAKES A STAND

O ***THIS DISAPPOINTMENT*** in the visitors' locker room at Boston Garden, where air-conditioning was the stuff of fantasy, was as thick as the humidity in the aftermath of the Bruins' 5–4 overtime victory over the Penguins in Game 2 of the Wales Conference Final. The star of the evening was Boston forward Vladimir Ruzicka, who set up his team's first four goals and then scored the game winner, but the postgame spotlight fell squarely on Pittsburgh winger Kevin Stevens. Although the sweat was pouring out of Stevens, pretty much reducing his white dress shirt to a new epidermis, he stood in the middle of the locker room and told wave after wave of reporters that even though the Bruins were favored in the series and had won the first two games, the outcome was far from settled. Or, more to the point, that the outcome was settled, but that it wasn't what almost everyone was anticipating. "We're confident we can beat this team," he said. "And we will beat this team. We'll beat this team. I'll say it right now, we'll beat them." His tone was forceful, his message bold and brazen. And, as it turned out, 100 percent accurate.

MAY 11, 1991

TAKING THE NEXT STEP

THE PENGUINS covered a lot of new territory during the 1990–91 season. Won a division for the first time. Made their initial foray past Round 2 of the playoffs. And then captured a conference championship. They did the latter in an improbable way, running off four consecutive victories against Boston after dropping Games 1 and 2 of the Wales Conference Final. The clincher came in a 5–3 victory in Game 6 at the Civic Arena, but it was not a game in which the outcome was a foregone conclusion. The Bruins took an early 2–0 lead, and even Bob Johnson, the Penguins' chronically optimistic coach, allowed that "When it was 2–0, it looked like it was going to be one of those nights." But Larry Murphy and Phil Bourque scored to pull the Penguins even. "The goals they got actually seemed to wake us up," Penguins goalie Tom Barrasso said. And then the Penguins began to assert their will. Mark Recchi got what turned out to be the series winner when he chased down a Gordie Roberts pass and beat Boston goalie Andy Moog from above the right dot at 15:40 of the third period. "I had a pretty good feeling when I shot it," Recchi said. And an ever better one when it got by Moog. Mario Lemieux sealed Pittsburgh's place in the Stanley Cup Final with an empty-net goal.

In a series of firsts, the Penguins added another by claiming the championship of the Wales Conference.
COURTESY OF GETTY IMAGES

Mario Lemieux's goal in Game 2 of the 1991 Stanley Cup Final was one of his very best. COURTESY OF GETTY IMAGES

MAY 17, 1991

LEMIEUX MAKES IT LOOK EASY

MARIO LEMIEUX did some of his best work on the biggest stages, whether it was scoring the title-winning goal for Canada against the Soviet Union in the 1987 Canada Cup tournament or authoring the signature goal of his pro career in Game 2 of the 1991 Stanley Cup Final against Minnesota. The Penguins were protecting a 2–1 lead late in the second period when Phil Bourque passed the puck to Lemieux in the Penguins' zone. Lemieux carried the puck through center ice and into the Minnesota end, then burst between North Stars defensemen Neil Wilkinson and Shawn Chambers. After putting the puck between Chambers's skates, Lemieux bore down on goalie Jon Casey and slid a backhander into the net while falling to the ice after Casey made a futile attempt to poke the puck away from him. "A great play by a great player," Pittsburgh coach Bob Johnson said after his team's 4–1 victory. No one disputed that, although Lemieux seemed to see it mostly as trying to perform to the level expected by his bosses. "That's why they pay me a lot of money," he said.

MAY 25, 1991

CHAMPIONS AT LAST

WINNING A Stanley Cup isn't supposed to be easy, and it wasn't for the Penguins in 1991. They only made it look that way, at least in their title-clinching 8–0 victory over Minnesota at the Met Center in Bloomington, Minnesota. Rugged defenseman Ulf Samuelsson gave them the only goal they would need two minutes into the opening period, but his teammates would add seven more, just to make sure. And when the third period ended at 10:48 p.m. Eastern, the Penguins were sitting alone atop the hockey world for the first time in their history. "It's a great thrill to reach the top of the mountain," coach Bob Johnson said. All 24 players the Penguins used during their four-round slog to the championship contributed, no one more than Mario Lemieux—who had 16 goals and 28 assists to earn the Conn Smythe Trophy as playoff MVP and who was suitably moved by what he and his teammates had accomplished. "There are guys who play 10 or 15 years in the league and never get a chance to participate in the Final," Lemieux said. "The feeling is unbelievable." Winning the Cup was especially satisfying for veterans like Bob Errey, Troy Loney, and Phil Bourque, who had been with the organization since the days when it was wandering through the hockey wilderness, looking like a team that would never get back into the playoffs, let alone be the only club standing when a postseason ended. "I never would have expected this in a million years," Loney said. If anything, Bourque was even more effusive. "This is the best thing that ever happened to me," he said. Perhaps the sentiment on that most heady of nights was best expressed by rookie defenseman Jim Paek, who said simply, "Don't ever wake me up."

The franchise's long Stanley Cup drought ended on a May evening in Bloomington, Minnesota. COURTESY OF GETTY IMAGES

Paul Coffey's skating and skill made him an offensive weapon with few equals among NHL defensemen.
COURTESY OF GETTY IMAGES

OCTOBER 17, 1991

COFFEY BREWS SOME HISTORY

HOW GOOD of an offensive defenseman was Paul Coffey? Good enough that he became the NHL's all-time leading point producer at his position by shooting wide of an opponent's net. Coffey threw a shot toward New York Islanders goalie Glenn Healy during the third period of the Penguins' 8–5 victory at the Civic Arena, and the puck sailed wide of the target. However, left winger Bob Errey collected the rebound and beat Healy, giving Coffey an assist and his 1,053rd point in the league, moving him one ahead of Islanders legend Denis Potvin. "A record like that is hard to believe," coach Scott Bowman said. After the game, Coffey joked about failing to get his shot on goal. "That was the only play I had," he said. "I had to shoot wide and have [Errey] pick it up and come around and score." That wasn't the only one of Potvin's records that Coffey broke in the game—his two assists gave him 744 in his first 815 NHL games, while Potvin had 742 in 1,060—but understandably, the focus was on Coffey becoming the highest-scoring defenseman to play in the league. "It's kind of hard to believe, coming from a small town [Weston, Ontario] and putting those kinds of numbers up," Coffey said. "Passing two great hockey players in Bobby Orr and, of course, Denis Potvin. It's a nice feeling."

NOVEMBER 26, 1991

A LEGEND LEAVES US

BOB JOHNSON, who ranks among the most beloved individuals in franchise history, died at his home in Colorado Springs just under three months after he was diagnosed with brain cancer while preparing Team USA to compete in the Canada Cup tournament. General manager Craig Patrick delivered news of Johnson's death to the team after it completed a practice under Scotty Bowman, who had moved behind the bench from his position in the front office after Johnson was stricken. And while Johnson's players had heard for weeks that his prospects for beating the disease were slim at best, they nonetheless seemed stunned to find out that he had passed away. "You hear he's struggling and so on, yet even though you somewhat expect this to happen, it still hits you over the head like a hammer," center Ron Francis said. "I don't know how it's going to affect us [on the ice]. We're all human beings. We all feel pain, and this certainly is a painful time for everyone." Johnson, who was renowned for his unwavering optimism and whose oft-stated observation that "It's a great day for hockey" would become an enduring mantra for the franchise, was honored with a candlelight ceremony at the Civic Arena the night after he died, before the Penguins faced New Jersey.

Bob Johnson's death from brain cancer was a devastating blow to Penguins players, staff, and fans.
COURTESY OF GETTY IMAGES

DECEMBER 26, 1991

MULLEN GETS FOUR-SQUARED

JOE MULLEN entered the NHL's holiday break in style, scoring four goals in the Penguins' 6–3 victory on Long Island in their final game before they got a couple of days off. He apparently decided that more of the same would be a good way to get going when the Penguins came out of the break, so he scored four more in a 12–1 victory over Toronto in a game that might not have been as close as the score suggested. "It was embarrassing, to say the least," Toronto general manager Cliff Fletcher said. The Penguins, understandably, had a somewhat different perspective on how the evening played out. "It was crazy out there," said left winger Kevin Stevens, who was playing on a line with Mullen and Mario Lemieux. "One of those nights where everything went in the net." Especially when Mullen shot it, which was no surprise to Fletcher, who had been GM in Calgary when the Flames traded Mullen to Pittsburgh. "One thing about Joey," he said. "If he gets an opportunity, you know where the puck's going." Well, much of the time, anyway. But while Mullen, who scored the Penguins' first, second, ninth, and 10th goals against Maple Leafs goaltender Grant Fuhr, wasn't complaining about shooting 8-for-11 from the field in those two games, he suggested he actually could have done better. "I'm getting a lot of opportunities," he said. "I even missed a couple in both this game and the last one. And they were real good chances, too."

Although the spotlight rarely fell on Joe Mullen, he was a consistent, prolific point producer and two-way player.
COURTESY OF GETTY IMAGES

Penguins players didn't make up the entire Wales Conference squad at the 1992 All-Star Game. It just seemed that way.
COURTESY OF GETTY IMAGES

JANUARY 18, 1992

A CONSTELLATION OF PENGUINS

THE PENGUINS practically turned the 1992 NHL All-Star Game into an intrasquad scrimmage. Although the game was held in Philadelphia, the Wales Conference lineup had a decidedly Western Pennsylvania flavor as no fewer than four Penguins—Mario Lemieux, Paul Coffey, Kevin Stevens, and Jaromir Jagr—were named starters and Bryan Trottier was added in the veterans category. What's more, Pittsburgh coach Scotty Bowman was working behind the Wales bench. Despite having strength in numbers, the Penguins didn't have a major impact on the outcome, a 10–6 Campbell Conference victory. Stevens, who played the entire game on a line with Lemieux and Jagr, had a goal, as did Trottier, but St. Louis winger Brett Hull scored twice for the winners to earn the MVP award. Hull was being fed passes by linemate-for-a-day Wayne Gretzky, who said, "I just want to get him the puck." Seemed like a reasonable plan. Washington goalie Don Beaupre, who gave up six Campbell goals on 12 shots in 20 minutes of action, had to settle for getting nothing more than a little sympathy for being victimized in a game that annually put a heavy emphasis on offense. "For a while, it seemed like everything was going by me," he said, adding, "I knew eventually they would hit me with one."

FEBRUARY 19, 1992

COFFEY, RECCHI SHIPPED OUT

CRAIG PATRICK, who had pulled off one of the most important trades in franchise history when he acquired Ron Francis, Ulf Samuelsson, and Grant Jennings from Hartford about 10-and-a-half months earlier, tried to replicate his success from that deal with an even bigger one in a three-team swap with Los Angeles and Philadelphia that brought Rick Tocchet, Kjell Samuelsson, Ken Wregget, and Jeff Chychrun to the Penguins at the cost of Paul Coffey, Mark Recchi, Brian Benning, and a first-round draft choice. The Penguins were defending Stanley Cup champions, but they had been sputtering through the regular season and Patrick determined that they would benefit from upgrading their defensive play with Samuelsson and Chychrun and from adding some badly needed muscle and grit in the form of Tocchet. "Our objective was to improve our team defensively and to improve our physical presence on the ice," Patrick said. "We wanted to improve our chances to repeat as Stanley Cup champions." The trade initially was met with mixed reviews in Pittsburgh, mostly because losing Coffey and Recchi created obvious holes in the Penguins' lineup. Ultimately, however, the moves Patrick made with the Flyers and Kings turned out to pay off the way his trade with Hartford had, as the Penguins captured the Cup again a few months later, with Tocchet and Samuelsson playing particularly important roles and Wregget proving to be an excellent goaltending partner for Tom Barrasso.

Craig Patrick jolted his lineup by trading away Mark Recchi and Paul Coffey and adding Rick Tocchet, Kjell Samuelsson, and Ken Wregget. COURTESY OF GETTY IMAGES

MARCH 24, 1992

IS IT HISTORY IF NO ONE NOTICES?

Kevin Stevens did some remarkable things during his time together with Mario Lemieux.
COURTESY OF GETTY IMAGES

MARIO LEMIEUX made headlines and history with trip-hammer regularity for most of his time in pro hockey, so perhaps it was predictable that some of his feats would be overlooked—or, at the very least, overshadowed at times. And so it was when he became the second-fastest player in league history to put up 1,000 career points, picking up a goal and an assist in a 4–3 loss at Joe Louis Arena in Detroit. It was the Red Wings' first win against Pittsburgh in 12 games, and it was Lemieux's 513th game. (Wayne Gretzky set the NHL record by getting 1,000 points in 424 games.) Lemieux's accomplishment seemed to be pretty much an afterthought following the game, perhaps because his landmark assist came on a Kevin Stevens goal that swelled his total for the season to 50. Because that puck represented a milestone achievement for both players, it wasn't immediately clear which one would be given custody of it. "I guess we're going to have to cut it in half," Stevens said. Which player would get to display that puck in his trophy case wasn't the primary concern for anyone on this night, however. Not when losing to the Red Wings mathematically eliminated the Penguins from challenging for second place in the Patrick Division. And not when their power play, which should have been a formidable weapon, was in a drought and had looked bad while accomplishing little. "Everything's not working on it," Stevens said. "I don't think there's one good thing that we're doing."

MAY 5, 1992

RANGERS TAKE OUT LEMIEUX, MULLEN

LOSING GAME 2 in the second round to the New York Rangers was bad. Losing two of their top players, Mario Lemieux and Joe Mullen, in the first period of that game was a lot worse for the Penguins. They were on a power play at 5:05 of the opening period when New York's Adam Graves slashed Lemieux's left hand, knocking him out of the game (and, as it turned out, the series). Although he acknowledged slashing Lemieux, Graves insisted he did so with no malintent. "When you're penalty-killing, you try to put pressure on the guy's hands to move the puck, for him to give up the puck so you can shoot it down the ice," he said. "It wasn't an intent to hurt him. In no way would I want to hurt him." Referee Dan Marouelli only assessed a minor penalty to Graves, who was suspended for the balance of the series after a league review of the incident. Already down a key forward, the Penguins lost another late in the period, when New York's Kris King delivered a forearm to the head of Mullen, who could not avoid it because he was off-balance because he was stepping over a leg extended by Rangers forward Paul Broten. Mullen suffered a knee injury that had to be surgically repaired and ended his season. Despite that early adversity, Pittsburgh took a 2–1 lead into the third period, but New York ran off three unanswered goals to even the series, 1–1.

Losing Mario Lemieux and Joe Mullen seemed like it might be a mortal blow to the Penguins' chances of repeating as champions.
COURTESY OF GETTY IMAGES

Larry Murphy's timely steal made Ron Francis's overtime game-winner against the New York Rangers possible.
COURTESY OF GETTY IMAGES

MAY 9, 1992

FRANCIS TO THE RESCUE

THE PENGUINS were in a pretty precarious spot heading into Game 4 of their second-round series against the New York Rangers. New York had won two of the first three games, and the Penguins were without Mario Lemieux and Joe Mullen, both injured in Game 2. So when New York built a 3–1 lead midway through the second period, the Penguins' prospects for successfully defending the Stanley Cup they'd won a year earlier began to dim. At least until Ron Francis beat New York goalie Mike Richter with a harmless-looking shot from just outside the Rangers' blue line. The puck glanced off Richter's glove before settling in the net. Although that revived the Penguins, as well as the sellout crowd of 16,164 at the Civic Arena, Mark Messier restored New York's two-goal cushion early in the third. That meant the Penguins needed two more goals just to make the game an overtime toss-up. Francis got the first of those at 10:27, and Troy Loney converted a Jaromir Jagr feed 85 seconds later. That closed out the scoring in regulation, and Francis put an exclamation point on the Penguins' comeback victory during a power play at 2:47 of the extra period. Defenseman Larry Murphy triggered the game-deciding sequence by stealing the puck from Messier and throwing it toward Rangers goalie John Vanbiesbrouck, who had replaced Richter after Loney's goal. Francis got his stick on the shot, and the puck slid inside the left post to tie the series, 2–2.

MAY 23, 1992

PENGUINS SWEEP TO ANOTHER WALES TITLE

THERE WAS some real suspense about how the rematch between the Penguins and Boston in the 1992 Wales Conference Final would play out. At least until Jaromir Jagr's goal at 9:44 of overtime gave the Penguins a 4–3 victory in Game 1. After that, the Penguins' return to the Stanley Cup Final was pretty much a formality, as they beat the Bruins in four consecutive games, including a pair of 5–1 victories in Games 3 and 4 at Boston Garden. Boston native and nemesis Kevin Stevens led the charge by scoring four times in Game 3, and Mario Lemieux (two), Jagr, Paul Stanton, and Dave Michayluk deposited pucks behind Boston goalie Andy Moog in the series finale. Lemieux, who did not play in the series opener, and Jagr, who had a second goal waved off in the first period of the series finale because referee Don Koharski ruled that the Boston net had been dislodged before Jagr's shot crossed the goal line, shared the team lead with eight points in the series, while Lemieux and Stevens each had a team-high four goals. Lemieux scored a signature goal while killing a penalty in the opening period of Game 4, carrying the puck from the Penguins' zone and into the Boston end before putting it between the legs of Bruins defenseman Raymond Bourque and collecting it on the other side before beating Moog for what would go down as the game winner.

Jaromir Jagr helped the Penguins get by Boston in the Wales Conference Final for the second year in a row. COURTESY OF GETTY IMAGES

MAY 26, 1992

A COMEBACK FOR THE AGES

CHICAGO TOOK a playoff-record 11-game winning streak into Game 1 of the Stanley Cup Final at the Civic Arena, which was more than enough to get the Penguins' attention. And if it hadn't been, seeing the Blackhawks build a 4–1 lead by 11:36 of the second period on goals by Chris Chelios, Michel Goulet, Dirk Graham, and Duane Sutter surely would have done it. The Penguins didn't seem fazed, though, and went about pulling off one of the most storied in-game comebacks in team history. It began when Rick Tocchet beat Blackhawks goalie Ed Belfour at 15:24, and Mario Lemieux banked a shot off Belfour and into the net from behind the goal line 59 seconds later. The Penguins, however, could not manufacture a tying goal until 15:05 of the third, when Jaromir Jagr scored what Lemieux called "the greatest goal I've ever seen." Jagr got the puck along the left-wing boards, deked around Sutter, then cut across the ice and eluded defensemen Igor Kravchuk and Frantisek Kucera before tossing in a backhander from the right circle to make it 4–4. The game seemed headed to overtime, but Chicago defenseman Steve Smith was assessed a penalty for hooking Lemieux with 18 seconds left in regulation. With the Penguins on the power play, Ron Francis won a face-off, pulling the puck to Larry Murphy at the right point. Belfour stopped Murphy's wrist shot, but Lemieux pounced on the rebound and threw it into the net for the game winner with 12.6 seconds to play. "Even though it was the first game, I thought it was a pretty key game," Jagr said. To say nothing of a portent.

The Penguins' third-period comeback against Chicago in Game 1 of the 1992 Cup Final was nothing shy of epic. COURTESY OF GETTY IMAGES

The Penguins rolled to their second title in a row on the strength of an 11-game winning streak. COURTESY OF GETTY IMAGES

JUNE 1, 1992

REPEAT PERFORMANCE

THE PENGUINS completed their sweep of Chicago with a 6–5 victory in Game 4 at Chicago Stadium, giving them their second championship in two years. "When you win twice, it's no fluke," left winger Kevin Stevens said. Pittsburgh finished the postseason with 11 consecutive victories, tying the league record the Blackhawks set earlier that spring. Unlike Game 3, which had been a 1–0 Penguins win, the series finale was a virtual goalfest, with Ron Francis getting what proved to be the Cup winner at 7:59 of the third period. "We can play any game they want," Mario Lemieux said. Before Francis scored, Jaromir Jagr, Stevens, Lemieux, Rick Tocchet, and Larry Murphy had gotten goals for the Penguins, whose onslaught prompted Chicago coach Mike Keenan to replace starting goalie Ed Belfour with young, largely untested Dominik Hasek. Tom Barrasso, who recorded his only shutout during Pittsburgh's second Cup run in Game 3 of the Final, was in goal for all 11 games of the team's surge through the final two-plus rounds of the postseason. Penguins partisans were denied one of the cherished keepsakes of many fans when their club wins a championship—newspaper front pages celebrating the accomplishment—because the *Post-Gazette* editorial department was on strike and *The Pittsburgh Press*, using the masthead of the *Allegheny Bulletin*, was publishing on a severely restricted schedule due to a labor dispute that shut down all unionized parts of the papers' operations.

Mario Lemieux's cancer diagnosis shocked the hockey world in 1993.
COURTESY OF GETTY IMAGES

JANUARY 12, 1993

A DAUNTING DIAGNOSIS

MARIO LEMIEUX, who had dealt with a number of medical issues—most of them focused on his back—over the course of his career, announced at a press conference that he was facing a challenge more daunting than any he had taken on in the past: cancer. He had been diagnosed with Hodgkin's lymphoma, which attacks the immune system. Suddenly, things like Stanley Cups and scoring titles and individual honors didn't seem nearly so important. "It is scary," Lemieux said. "Anytime you hear the word *cancer*." While there was obvious and understandable concern for Lemieux's well-being, the early prognosis was quite encouraging. The condition had been caught early—Lemieux was examined after feeling a lump on his neck—which greatly enhanced the chances of a full recovery. His agent, Tom Reich, released a statement that said, "He has a condition . . . that is in a mild stage. The prognosis is extremely good." Despite the optimism, Lemieux's teammates didn't try to conceal their concern. "Anytime you're talking about cancer, you're worried," Bob Errey said. "You just have to trust what the doctors are saying and be positive." Some, especially those who had watched Lemieux deal with serious back problems, seemed shocked that yet another health-related hurdle had been placed in front of him. "I don't know what more that guy is going to have to go through," Troy Loney said. "I just feel for him. I couldn't care less when he comes back [to play], just that he gets healthy."

MARCH 2, 1993

HE HAD EVERYTHING BUT A CAPE

ALTHOUGH MARIO LEMIEUX made a number of stunning comebacks over the course of his legendary career, the one he staged on this night topped all of the others. After sitting out 23 games while undergoing treatment for Hodgkin's disease, Lemieux recorded a goal and an assist in a 5–4 loss in Philadelphia. And that was among the least-surprising developments of the day, considering that Lemieux received a warm ovation from the usually hostile crowd at the Spectrum and that simply making it across the state that day was a feat. And it all happened just hours after Lemieux received his 22nd and final radiation treatment. He was booked on a commercial flight from Pittsburgh to Philadelphia at 10 a.m., but the plane was fogged in in Chicago. After it was delayed for the fourth time, Lemieux arranged for a private flight to get him to Philadelphia. He landed on the far side of the Commonwealth around 1 p.m., got a little rest at the team hotel, then reported to work as if it were just another day (except that he was wearing a black turtleneck under his game sweater). And while Lemieux wasn't particularly impressed by how he performed after his extended layoff, saying only that "it felt good to be back," his teammates weren't nearly as reserved. "How can you even imagine what he did tonight?" linemate Kevin Stevens said. "There's only one person in the world who could do it, and it's him."

Mario Lemieux did many amazing things during his career. His performance after beating cancer might have been the best.
COURTESY OF GETTY IMAGES

The Penguins earned a place in the league record book by humbling the New York Rangers at Madison Square Garden. COURTESY OF GETTY IMAGES

APRIL 9, 1993

GOOD TIMES AT THE GARDEN

THE PENGUINS of 1992–93 had a flair for the spectacular, and nothing illustrated that better than the night they set an NHL record by winning their 16th consecutive game. They overwhelmed the New York Rangers, 10–4, at Madison Square Garden, with (who else?) Mario Lemieux leading the way by scoring five times, all in the final two periods, on New York goalies Corey Hirsch and Mike Richter. "He was on a different level tonight," Pittsburgh forward Shawn McEachern said. "I think everything he touched was going in the net." It only seemed that way, since Hirsch and Richter actually managed to reject three of the pucks Lemieux threw at them. Of course, their teammates had as woeful an evening as those goaltenders did, because the Penguins trampled them for most of the evening. "Great teams do that," Lemieux said. "They go out there and do whatever it takes to win. This is the best team I ever played with. We have three lines that can score a lot of goals, a lot of guys who can put the puck in the net. It's pretty tough to find, guys who can score 30, 40, 50 goals, which we have on every line." As if to reinforce Lemieux's point, Joe Mullen had a hat trick against the Rangers. The Penguins' victory broke the record set by the New York Islanders in 1982, when the Islanders' run of 15 wins in a row had been snapped by Pittsburgh.

APRIL 14, 1993

LEMIEUX'S CROWNING ACHIEVEMENT

THAT MARIO LEMIEUX was able to come back from cancer and perform as if he had never missed a shift was impressive enough, but what he accomplished during the balance of the 1992–93 regular season was nothing shy of incredible. Which probably is understating it. When he returned to active duty, Lemieux trailed Buffalo Sabres center Pat LaFontaine, a future Hall of Famer himself, by a dozen points in the NHL scoring race. When the Penguins closed out their regular season with a 6–6 tie at New Jersey, Lemieux had locked up his fourth Art Ross Trophy as the league's top point-producer with a 12-point cushion over LaFontaine, despite appearing in 24 fewer games. Lemieux's post-Hodgkin's surge included an 11-game streak during which he scored 21 goals. He would finish the season with two or more points in an incredible 48 of the 60 games in which he appeared. "The biggest surprise [of the season] was the play of Mario and the team after his return [from the cancer treatments]," coach Scotty Bowman said. Center Ron Francis echoed that sentiment. "For . . . him to do what he's done since he's come back, it was just a fantastic finish," he said. Truth be told, though, Lemieux's finish really was nothing more than a perfect bookend to his start. When his layoff because of the radiation treatments began, he had put up 39 goals and 65 assists in 40 games.

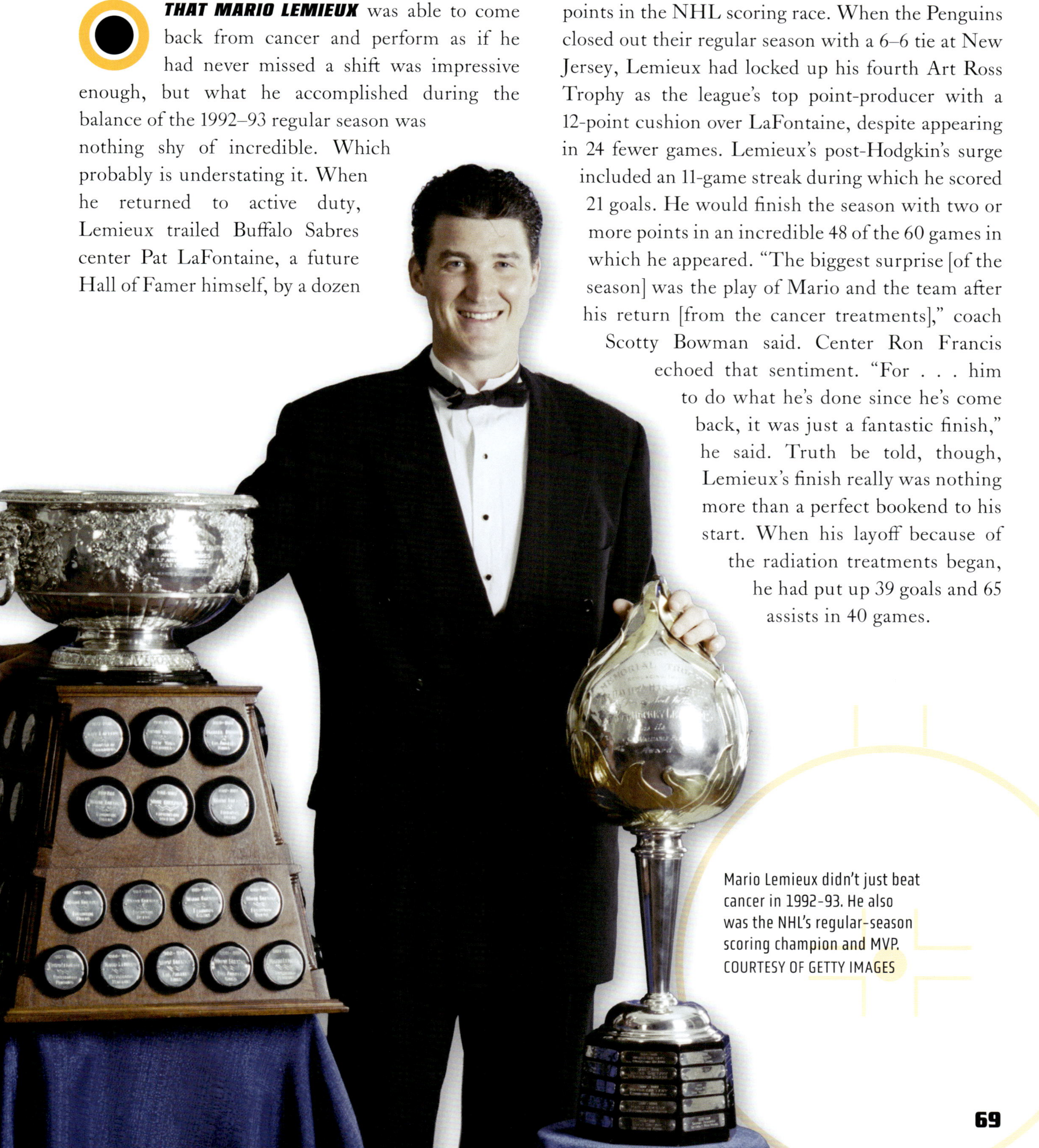

Mario Lemieux didn't just beat cancer in 1992-93. He also was the NHL's regular-season scoring champion and MVP. COURTESY OF GETTY IMAGES

The Penguins closed out the 1992-93 regular season on a 17-0-1 roll. COURTESY OF GETTY IMAGES

APRIL 14, 1993

THE TOP OF THE MOUNTAIN

THE PENGUINS closed out their only Presidents' Trophy–winning season as the NHL's best regular-season team with a rather forgettable 6–6 tie at Brendan Byrne Arena in New Jersey, but they were able to secure their 119th point of 1992–93 when Joe Mullen scored on Devils goalie Craig Billington with 66 seconds remaining in regulation. That was the only goal the Penguins scored all season after replacing their goalie with an extra attacker, perhaps because they didn't make a habit of being behind late in games. The Penguins played the final 10-plus minutes of regulation without right winger Rick Tocchet, who was assessed a match penalty for head-butting New Jersey defenseman Scott Niedermayer. When the final buzzer sounded at the Meadowlands, the Penguins had set franchise records not only for points, but for a variety of statistics ranging from victories (56) to 100-point scorers (four) to road wins (24). "There were a lot of bright spots in this season," defenseman Larry Murphy said. "It's tough to point to one. I'd say winning the Presidents' Trophy would be, but we won it a couple of weeks before the end of the season, so it was really kind of anticlimactic." That doesn't mean that all the Penguins were able to accomplish between October and April wasn't extraordinary. "It's tough to get over 100 points in our league, and we did it easily," Mario Lemieux said. The Penguins entered the playoffs a few days later without a loss since March 5.

MAY 14, 1993

THE THREE-PEAT DREAM DIES

THE PENGUINS entered the 1993 playoffs as near-prohibitive favorites to win the Stanley Cup, and understandably so. After all, they were defending two-time champions and had been the NHL's dominant force in the just-completed regular season. And when they dispatched New Jersey in just five games during Round 1 of the postseason, there wasn't much reason to believe that their bid for another title was in trouble. But then the New York Islanders showed up. New York had stunned the Penguins 18 years earlier by rallying from a 3–0 deficit to win a best-of-seven series, and they pulled an even bigger shocker this time as they battled the Penguins—who had finished 32 points ahead of them during the regular season—ferociously and took the series to a seventh game—then stunned the Penguins and the capacity crowd of 16,164 at the Civic Arena by getting a decisive goal from David Volek at 5:16 of overtime. Volek launched the Islanders into the Wales Conference Final against Montreal by beating Penguins goalie Tom Barrasso to cap an odd-man break after the Penguins got goals from Ron Francis and Rick Tocchet during the final four minutes of regulation to push the game past the third period. Turned out all they did was to give their team a stay of execution. "Winning is a tremendous feeling and once you start doing it, you never want to stop," Barrasso said. "When you're on top, you feel invincible. And right now, we're obviously not there anymore."

The New York Islanders' David Volek ended the Penguins' dream of winning three Stanley Cups in a row.
COURTESY OF GETTY IMAGES

MAY 28, 1993

SCOTTY BOWMAN DEPARTS

WHEN THE PENGUINS wrapped up their regular-season schedule with a 6–6 tie in New Jersey on April 14, Scotty Bowman said he was "well-satisfied with my [contract] arrangement in Pittsburgh" and that it "would take a major-major change" for him to leave the Penguins during the offseason. General manager Craig Patrick said Bowman's agreement with the Penguins afforded him the option of returning as coach, serving as a consultant, or becoming director of player recruitment and development. Oh, and there was one other possibility: leaving. And that's the path Bowman, the winningest coach in NHL history, chose to follow by declining to meet a deadline Patrick imposed for letting the Penguins know if he was interested in returning. "He is not prepared to make a decision on whether he wants to coach our team or not," Patrick said. "For that reason, we're going in another direction." Patrick's hard-line approach seemed to be a by-product of protracted, sometimes acrimonious negotiations with Bowman a year earlier, when Patrick was trying to convince him to spend a second season behind the Penguins' bench. "I don't think our organization should go through that again," he said. "We did it once. Once is enough." Although Patrick left the door open for Bowman to take on one of the other positions—"He can come back in one of the other two capacities," Patrick said. "Not as coach."—Bowman accepted an offer to take over as coach of the Detroit Red Wings.

Scotty Bowman, the winningest coach in NHL history, left the Penguins after spending two seasons behind their bench.
COURTESY OF GETTY IMAGES

FEBRUARY 16, 1995

OFF TO A FLYING START

THE BEGINNING of the NHL season was delayed several months by a labor dispute, but when it finally got underway the Penguins hit the ground running. No, make that sprinting. Their 5–2 victory over Hartford made them 12–0, with one tie, in their first 13 games, their best-ever start to a season and the third-best in league history. That was all the more noteworthy because the Penguins were without Mario Lemieux, who had announced during the summer that he planned to sit out the season. Lemieux's absence was particularly disappointing for left winger Luc Robitaille, who had been acquired from Los Angeles during the offseason and was hoping to work alongside Lemieux. Coincidentally or otherwise, Robitaille—one of the premier goal-scorers of his generation—didn't hit the net as often as he wanted during his first dozen games in Pittsburgh. He broke out of that slump in a big way against the Whalers, however, scoring four times, after which he insisted he wasn't concerned about his relatively modest productivity. "You always want to do well," he said. "But we kept winning, so it doesn't really matter." Robitaille's goals left him one shy of 400 in his career, which helps to explain why coach Eddie Johnston wasn't concerned that Robitaille's scoring touch had deserted him. "I worry when a guy doesn't get chances," he said. "But he's hit a few goalposts and missed a couple of open nets. You know the tide's going to change for a guy like that."

Luc Robitaille and Jaromir Jagr helped the Penguins to a strong start in the lockout-delayed 1995 season. COURTESY OF GETTY IMAGES

Mario Lemieux marked the birth of his son, Austin, in style by scoring five times against St. Louis. COURTESY OF GETTY IMAGES

MARCH 26, 1996

ALL IN THE FAMILY

SOME MEN celebrate the birth of a child by handing out cigars. Mario Lemieux opted to mark the arrival of his son, Austin, who was born several months prematurely, by scoring five goals in an 8–4 win over St. Louis at Mellon Arena. Lemieux acknowledged that focusing on hockey had been a challenge for a while, and his relief was evident in his play. "It's been very difficult for myself and my family the last couple of months," he said. "By the way I was playing, I think everybody knew something was up. I was not able to play very well. I think my head was somewhere else." If so, Lemieux seemed intent on making up for it in one night, as he punctuated his big night by setting up a couple of the goals that he didn't score, pushing his career assists total to 800. It was the 37th hat trick of Lemieux's career and his third five-goal game. Perhaps the most striking thing was that Lemieux said after the game that he "could have had a couple more." He scored his first goal at 3:35 of the opening period and added another before the first intermission to give the Penguins a 3–2 lead. He chipped in another pair of goals in the second period and his fifth at 6:08 of the third, leaving him one shy of the NHL single-game record. "I've had five a few times," he said. "But I was trying to get the sixth one."

APRIL 24, 1996

NEDVED GETS A TIMELY GOAL

THE PENGUINS had never played into four overtimes before Game 4 of their opening-round series with Washington at USAir Arena in Landover, Maryland. And they haven't played a game quite like their 3–2 victory since. It didn't end until 2:16 a.m., when Petr Nedved beat Capitals goalie Olaf Kolzig from above the left dot with 44.6 seconds to go before the seventh intermission to complete Pittsburgh's comeback from a 2–0 deficit and tie the series, 2–2. It was, at that point, the third-longest game in league history, and surely one of the most eventful. Consider that Penguins center Mario Lemieux was ejected from the game when he picked up 19 penalty minutes at 19:23 of the second period for jumping on Washington's Todd Krygier and pummeling him after Krygier had attempted to pitchfork Lemieux and had thrown a punch at him. Krygier received just one minor penalty, but teammate Pat Peake got a roughing minor and game misconduct for intervening on Krygier's behalf. Lemieux got minors for roughing and instigating, a fighting major, and a game misconduct. A few hours after Lemieux left the game, Penguins goalie Ken Wregget—who had replaced Tom Barrasso at the start of the second period—denied Washington forward Joe Juneau on a penalty shot. "I got lucky," Wregget said. "The puck bounced up on him, and he really didn't get much wood on it. . . . It could have very easily been over right there."

Petr Nedved's goal in the fourth overtime gave the Penguins a happy ending to one of the longest games they've played.
COURTESY OF GETTY IMAGES

JANUARY 15, 1997

LALIME COULDN'T LOSE

PATRICK LALIME was an unlikely candidate to scrawl his name in the NHL record book. He had been a sixth-round draft choice in 1993 and put in two seasons in the minors before playing a game for the Penguins, and he spent three more years bouncing around the International Hockey League after his rookie season with Pittsburgh. During what proved to be his only season with Pittsburgh, he put together the longest unbeaten streak at the start of a season by any rookie in the league. Lalime earned his niche in NHL history by stopping all 31 shots the Whalers threw at him in a 3–0 Penguins victory at the Hartford Civic Center to run his record to 13-0-2. "I was no more nervous (than usual)," Lalime said. He admitted, though, that he made sure to get a souvenir of the occasion as time was about to expire in the third period. "They shot the puck right at me at the end," he said. "I just grabbed it." While Lalime took his exceptional start—which he made the best for any Penguins goalie two nights later with a 4–2 win against Calgary—pretty much in stride, Mario Lemieux had a good perspective on its magnitude. After all, he had grown up in Montreal and watched Ken Dryden's remarkable play for the Canadiens. "He won five or six Stanley Cups and was the best in the world at the time," Lemieux said. "He was one of the greatest of all time."

Goalie Patrick Lalime's NHL career got off to a start that he never could have imagined.
COURTESY OF GETTY IMAGES

JANUARY 26, 1997

WHAT A HOMECOMING

MARIO LEMIEUX was Montreal's favorite son throughout his career, and the people there were always as excited to see him as Lemieux was to return to his hometown. But during his first decade-plus as a pro, Lemieux never put on a truly virtuoso performance—the kind that people who witness it talk about for decades. Not until this game, when he scored four times in the third period of a 5–2 Pittsburgh victory. It was the first time he'd scored more than two in 30 career games against the Canadiens, the team for which he rooted while growing up. He said it was "by far, the best game I've ever played here," and the crowd of 21,273 didn't seem inclined to argue the point. Certainly, Pittsburgh coach Eddie Johnston wasn't. "Amazing," Johnston said. "Just amazing. . . . He was flying all night. He could have had three or four more." Lemieux's hat trick was his second of the season and 39th in the NHL, tying him with Mike Bossy for second place on the all-time list behind Wayne Gretzky (49). "He just came and showed that he's the man," goalie Patrick Lalime said. Lemieux had made it known that he intended to step away from the game at the end of the season, so his chances to put on a show for the home folks were dwindling. "For him to come in here and put together a game like that, it's great to see," Ron Francis said.

Mario Lemieux put on a third-period performance that people in his hometown of Montreal won't forget for a long time.
COURTESY OF GETTY IMAGES

MARCH 4, 1997

MULLEN GETS NO. 500

JOE MULLEN rarely got the recognition he deserved for being the high-impact player that he was. Some of his accomplishments, though, simply could not be overlooked. Like when he became the first US-born player in NHL history to score 500 goals, which he did in a 6–3 loss to Colorado at McNichols Arena in Denver. "It's nice to get it over with," Mullen said. "It's a big relief." He got number 500 by deflecting a Chris Tamer shot past Avalanche goalie Patrick Roy at 16:01 of the second period, giving the Penguins a short-lived 3–2 lead. Trouble was, Colorado ran off four unanswered goals to close out the scoring. "It was exciting because we got the lead on the goal I scored," Mullen said. "Unfortunately, it didn't hold up. If we'd won, I'd be smiling a little more." Mullen already had joined the ranks of the league's previous 500-goal men, at least in one sense. Before the game, he had autographed some shirts the earlier members of the 500 Club had signed. "There were a couple of shirts with 500 goal-scorers on it," he said. "They were Michel Goulet's jerseys: one from Chicago, one from Quebec. He wanted me to sign it before the game. I was reluctant to do it, but [Penguins equipment manager Steve Latin] said they were very insistent. I asked if I could do it after the game, but they said it was worth too much money to keep around, so I did it."

There was no overlooking Joe Mullen on the night he scored his 500th career goal.
COURTESY OF GETTY IMAGES

It seemed only fitting that Mario Lemieux, Ron Francis, and Joe Mullen hit milestones in the same game.
COURTESY OF GETTY IMAGES

MARCH 29, 1997

GREAT THINGS COME IN THREES

HAVING RON Francis score his 400th career goal in a 4–1 victory over Los Angeles at the Civic Arena would have made the game memorable enough. But Francis's feat completed a hat trick of individual achievements that was unprecedented in the NHL, because it made the Penguins the first team to have players score their 400th, 500th (Joe Mullen), and 600th (Mario Lemieux) goals in the same season. "I've never really considered myself much of a goal-scorer," Francis said. "But to say I scored 400-plus goals in the National Hockey League is something to be proud of." Francis wasn't being immodest when he mentioned getting 400-plus goals in the league, because he already had scored number 401 against the struggling Kings. That he reached his milestone against Los Angeles didn't detract from Francis's accomplishment, but several Penguins players said they recognized only a few players on the visitors' bench. "Two of them," Jaromir Jagr said. "Kevin [Stevens] and Muzz [Glen Murray]." That wasn't saying much, considering that both were former teammates. But regardless of the opponent in this game, the Penguins figured they had to squeeze two points out of it because they had lost three games in a row and five of their previous seven. "We haven't exactly been tearing things up lately," Francis said. "So it was important for us to come out here and win a hockey game." Making a little history in the process was just a bonus. Particularly for Francis, Mullen, and Lemieux.

APRIL 26, 1997

MARIO LEMIEUX RETIRES . . . FOR A WHILE

ONE OF the most storied careers in NHL annals reached its conclusion—or so it seemed, anyway—when Mario Lemieux appeared in his final game, a 6–3 playoff loss at the CoreStates Center in Philadelphia. Lemieux scored one goal and set up another, but he didn't try to hide that his energy reserves had been depleted before the series even started. "It was awful for me," he said. "I didn't have my legs. I didn't have my strength. I just ran out of gas the last month of the season. . . . Not being able to play the way I once did is very frustrating for me. I just can't take that." That doesn't mean walking away from hockey was easy, as Lemieux realized as he was leaving the ice after Game 4 in Pittsburgh. "It was just a great moment," he said. "That was the first time I cried on the ice in a long time. When I came off, I started crying. It's the only time in my career that I did that. It was very emotional." Had Lemieux been inclined to weep when the series ended a few nights later, it might have been because he recognized how the Flyers had overwhelmed his team. "We just got overpowered," he said. True, but not before Philadelphia acknowledged his excellence one final time. "Hockey is going to miss Mario Lemieux," Flyers coach Terry Murray said. "He's been just a tremendous player for his whole career."

The greatest player in franchise history decided it was time to walk away from the game in 1997.
COURTESY OF GETTY IMAGES

JUNE 21, 1997

THE NHL COMES TO TOWN

IT TOOK until 30 years after Pittsburgh got its NHL franchise, but the city hosted an NHL Draft for the first time. The spotlight from across North America settled mostly on the likes of center Joe Thornton, claimed by Boston with the number one overall choice, and Patrick Marleau, who went to San Jose with the second pick. Locally, though, there was considerable attention paid to the Penguins' top pick, Slovak winger Robert Dome. He had spent the previous two years in the International Hockey League and was rated the number 27 prospect by NHL Central Scouting, but the Penguins took him with the 17th selection. Pittsburgh scouts were impressed by his powerful skating, and Dome apparently was, too, because he didn't balk before predicting, "I think I'm going to make the team." Well, he did appear in 30 NHL games that winter, scoring five times. Trouble is, he didn't get back to the league until two years later, when he got two goals in 22 games during his final go-round with the Penguins. He went on to appear in one more NHL game, with Calgary in 2002–03, before finishing his career in Europe. Happily for the Penguins, the draft wasn't a complete bust for them, because they picked up two defensemen—third-rounder Josef Melichar and eighth-rounder Andrew Ference—who spent considerable time in the NHL.

Hosting the 1997 NHL Draft allowed the Penguins to scratch another entry off their to-do list. COURTESY OF GETTY IMAGES

NOVEMBER 17, 1997

LEMIEUX, TROTTIER ENTER THE HALL

IN WHAT might be the ultimate statement on Mario Lemieux's talent and impact on the game, he was inducted to the Hockey Hall of Fame after the Hall made a rare exception to its rules and waived the standard three-year waiting period for players after they leave the game. That has been done only 10 times, always for some of the most accomplished and celebrated players to pass through the league. The others, in chronological order, are Dit Clapper, Maurice Richard, Ted Lindsay, Terry Sawchuk, Jean Beliveau, Gordie Howe, Red Kelly, Bobby Orr, and Wayne Gretzky. Lemieux's induction class included Bryan Trottier, who spent his final three seasons in Pittsburgh after winning four Stanley Cups with the New York Islanders. Lemieux described his induction as "the greatest honor I've ever received" and said it was "very special" that the Hall waived the normal waiting period for him. He was honored again two nights later, when he joined Michel Briere as the only players in franchise history to have their number retired.

Mario Lemieux joined Bryan Trottier in taking their place among the game's most celebrated and accomplished figures. COURTESY OF GETTY IMAGES

Ron Francis always was recognized for his exceptional defensive game, but still managed to hit a major offensive milestone. COURTESY OF GETTY IMAGES

MARCH 21, 1998

FRANCIS HITS 1,000

RON FRANCIS never sought attention, and he never got nearly as much as he deserved for being one of the finest two-way centers ever to play in the league. Some feats just couldn't be overlooked, however, like when he became the seventh player in NHL history to earn 1,000 career assists during a 4–3 victory over Philadelphia at the Civic Arena. Just how exclusive was that group? The other members were Wayne Gretzky, Gordie Howe, Marcel Dionne, Raymond Bourque, Paul Coffey, and Mark Messier. "That's quite a club to be able to say that you belong to," Francis said. He scrawled his signature in the record book at 18:22 of the second period, when he tossed a cross-ice pass to Fredrik Olausson, who drove a slap shot past Flyers goalie Ron Hextall from the top of the right circle. That sparked a lengthy standing ovation from the capacity crowd of 17,145. "I've been here a long time now and had a lot of great moments in front of these fans," Francis said. "And that certainly was one of the highlights."

JULY 13, 1998

FRANCIS LEAVES FOR CAROLINA

THE PENGUINS never doubted Ron Francis's value and importance to their team. They also never really believed that, after losing $37.5 million during the previous two years, that they could hold onto him when his contract expired. So bleak was their financial outlook that co-owner Howard Baldwin and GM Craig Patrick never had serious negotiations with Francis before he accepted a four-year, $20.8 million deal with Carolina. "I'm amazed at what some of the teams are spending," Baldwin said. "I think we've done a good job of keeping our top players here over the years, but it was tough to keep Ronnie at that price." Francis suggested it was equally difficult to leave, although the lack of meaningful contract talks made that inevitable. "What I had really wanted was to stay in Pittsburgh," he said. "It was a situation that I saw coming for the past year, and leaving there was a decision I was really dreading." Francis had entered the NHL with Carolina when that franchise was based in Hartford, and Hurricanes officials were delighted to be reunited with him. "We were able to get the best two-way player in the game," GM Jim Rutherford said. "And his leadership and his character fit into what we're trying to build here."

Howard Baldwin didn't have the resources to match the contract Carolina was willing to give Ron Francis. COURTESY OF GETTY IMAGES

OCTOBER 13, 1998

HERE WE GO AGAIN

IT WAS inevitable, really, and given the Penguins' checkered financial history, not even unprecedented. But for the second time in a little more than two decades, the team filed for bankruptcy, seeking Chapter 11 protection. Team officials hoped the move would help to smooth the path to a new arena; others were concerned it could put the Penguins on the road to another home. "Our reason for doing this was to keep the Penguins viable and in Pittsburgh," co-owner Roger Marino said. "When you're in protection, you're able to put money into the team rather than worrying about who else is going to come in and grab it. That's what this team needs right now, in the short term." Marino, who paid $40 million in 1997 to join the ownership group, estimated that he had put an additional $30 million into the franchise to keep it operational. Regardless of the uncertainty surrounding the future of the team, players insisted they were focused on their jobs. "There's not a guy on this team who's really paying any attention to that," right winger Rob Brown said. "We're here to play hockey, and that's it."

The ownership tandem of Roger Marino and Howard Baldwin had to declare bankruptcy.
© PITTSBURGH PENGUINS

Jaromir Jagr scored a lot of goals in the NHL, but one he got on Philadelphia's Ron Hextall probably stands above the rest.
COURTESY OF GETTY IMAGES

MARCH 13, 1999

JAGR OUTDOES HIMSELF

JAROMIR JAGR finished his NHL career with 766 goals in 1,733 regular-season games (assuming he doesn't decide to come out of retirement at, say, age 76), and more than a few of them were nothing less than breathtaking. But the one he scored during a 4–0 victory against Philadelphia goalie Ron Hextall at the Civic Arena was unlike any of the others. Or, perhaps, almost any that had been scored at any level of the game since the invention of artificial ice. It was early in the second period when Jagr charged through center ice, pulled in a pass from Martin Straka, and burst between Flyers defensemen Karl Dykhuis and Luke Richardson. Richardson knocked Jagr's legs out from under him as he moved down the slot, but Jagr was able to get off a backhander that Hextall saved. As Jagr was sliding toward the right post on his side, he knocked the rebound over Hextall's right shoulder. That gave the Penguins a 2–0 lead and the capacity crowd of 17,143 a memory that most fans would not soon forget. It certainly figured to stick with those who witnessed it from the Pittsburgh bench. "It was one of those you shake your head at and you say you're witnessing something that's going to be on the highlight reels forever, regarding one of the greatest goals ever scored," coach Kevin Constantine said. Jagr professed that it simply was a matter of good fortune. "Very lucky, that's all I can say," he said.

MAY 2, 1999

JAGR GIVES PENGUINS A LEG UP

THE PENGUINS were facing elimination when they met New Jersey in Game 6 of Round 1 in the Stanley Cup playoffs. Not just from postseason play, since the Devils held a 3–2 lead in the series, but from the Pittsburgh sporting landscape, since there was rampant speculation that the franchise might relocate. Jaromir Jagr was aware of all that, but he also knew that he was badly hobbled by a groin problem that had compelled him to sit out the previous four games. Badly enough that the Penguins weren't sure he'd even be able to dress for the game until after warm-ups. Turned out that Jagr didn't just play in the game; he authored an almost-unthinkable storyline for it. The Devils were protecting a 2–1 lead with a little more than two minutes left in regulation when Jagr, whose skating was obviously impaired by his groin issue, drove to the net and jammed a German Titov pass behind New Jersey goalie Martin Brodeur to force overtime. "It was kind of a lucky goal, but it went in," Jagr said. "It's the kind of goal you need in the playoffs." The Penguins also needed the one Jagr scored at 8:59 of overtime to send the series back to New Jersey for Game 7, as he lifted a shot over Brodeur after getting a feed from Martin Straka for the game winner. In the process, he added another chapter to his legendary career.

Few opponents found a way to shut down Jaromir Jagr. Turned out a serious groin injury couldn't do it, either.
COURTESY OF GETTY IMAGES

JUNE 24, 1999

NOW HE'S THE BOSS

MARIO LEMIEUX saved the Penguins when he joined the franchise in 1984, and he got a chance to do it again when a group of investors he headed won the right to buy the bankrupt club. "This is something we've been wanting for a long time," general manager Craig Patrick said. "In recent days, you could see that there were some positive things happening, and all of it finally came together." As part of the purchase agreement, Lemieux dropped a lawsuit over $32.5 million in deferred pay from his playing days against Roger Marino, who co-owned the team with Howard Baldwin. Lemieux was to convert $20 million of the $32.5 million into a stake in ownership and relinquish his claims to $7.5 million. Marino also was to give him another $5 million, an amount the club owed Marino. Lemieux had proven to be a commanding presence on the ice, but acknowledged that venturing into the business world as a team owner had its challenges. "I feel kind of like I did as a rookie when I was playing," he said. "I'm a little nervous, but I welcome the challenge. I absolutely think we can turn this around." Bold words from a guy who got involved only because he hadn't been paid the deferred money he was supposed to receive from the previous regime. "I have no regrets," Lemieux said. "For me, it was either leave town or defer the money. And I wasn't going to leave town. I'm a Pittsburgher."

Mario Lemieux saved the Penguins as a player, then came back to do it as an owner.
COURTESY OF GETTY IMAGES

JUNE 24, 1999

JAGR SHOWS HIS HART

On **MARIO LEMIEUX** taking over as owner of the Penguins was the biggest story of the day in Pittsburgh, but there was another that wasn't far behind: Jaromir Jagr received the Hart Trophy as the most valuable player in the NHL. It was the first time he won the Hart, but that wasn't all he took home from the league's awards ceremony at the Air Canada Centre in Toronto; he also got the Art Ross Trophy as the NHL's leading scorer and the Lester B. Pearson Award, which goes to the MVP as voted on by members of the NHL Players Association. "Three trophies," Jagr said. "It's unbelievable how lucky I've been today. Even when I was a little kid, I always dreamed of something big, of being the best player. This is the best feeling I've had since we won the Stanley Cup in 1991." Jagr was the clear choice for the Hart among the members of the Professional Hockey Writers Association who voted for it, grabbing the top spot on 51 of the 56 ballots cast. That put him comfortably ahead of the other finalists, Buffalo goalie Dominik Hasek and Ottawa center Alexei Yashin. Jagr admitted to being fired up about the honors bestowed on him—"When I score a goal, I get excited," he said. "And when I get a trophy like this, I get excited."

Jaromir Jagr returned from the 1999 NHL Awards ceremony with just about everything except an Oscar.
COURTESY OF GETTY IMAGES

The Penguins decided to move on from Tom Barrasso late in the 1999-2000 season.
COURTESY OF GETTY IMAGES

MARCH 14, 2000

BARRASSO GOES TO OTTAWA

CRAIG PATRICK was a busy man as the NHL trade deadline approached, pulling off five deals. That included one that ranked among the most significant in the league, as he sent goalie Tom Barrasso to Ottawa for goalie Ron Tugnutt and defenseman Janne Laukkanen. Barrasso had been one of just two players remaining from the Penguins' Stanley Cup–winning teams in 1991 and 1992; Jaromir Jagr was the other. Barrasso, arguably the most polarizing figure in team history because of his often-prickly personality, had to waive a no-trade clause to make it possible for the deal to go through, and Patrick admitted that he was reluctant to even broach the subject with him. "Quite frankly, I was afraid to call him . . . and maybe ruin him for the rest of the year," Patrick said. "We told him we wanted him to stay, but we wanted to let him know about this opportunity. He was open to it, and it worked out well for both sides." Barrasso was 5–7–2, with a 3.18 goals-against average, when he was traded. Neither Tugnutt nor Laukkanen had anticipated leaving the Senators with the stretch drive looming—and neither seemed particularly enthused about doing so. "I didn't expect it," said Tugnutt, who was Ottawa's all-time leader with 72 victories. "I guess [the Senators] feel they're doing the right thing for them, but I'm not so sure."

DECEMBER 27, 2000

AS IF HE NEVER LEFT

O**MARIO LEMIEUX** having a three-point game at Mellon Arena was such a common occurrence that it almost wasn't worth mentioning . . . except when he did it after returning from a three-and-a-half-year layoff. But that's precisely what happened on the night he came out of retirement, as Lemieux scored one goal and set up two others in a 5–0 victory against Toronto. "Even if he didn't score a point, just to come back after three years and play like that was unbelievable," Penguins forward Martin Straka said. "He just showed everyone he's the best player in the world, no matter what." Lemieux didn't actually own that distinction anymore; he had relinquished it to Penguins right winger Jaromir Jagr when he stepped away from hockey in 1997. But even Jagr admitted he didn't anticipate Lemieux's doing so much, so quickly, after not competing for so many winters. "I didn't know what was going to happen," Jagr said. "But I didn't expect anything like that." Jagr was the first beneficiary of Lemieux's comeback, as he converted a Lemieux pass 33 seconds after the opening face-off for his 20th goal of the season. Lemieux scored the 614th of his career in the middle of the second period, when he broke down the left side of the slot and beat Maple Leafs goalie Curtis Joseph after getting a pass from Jagr. He then set up Jan Hrinda, who was playing on a line with him and Jagr, about four minutes later to complete his personal linescore. "He could have had seven or eight points, easy," Straka said. "That was an awesome show."

Mario Lemieux made a major splash in his return to active duty after a three-and-a-half-year retirement.
COURTESY OF GETTY IMAGES

DECEMBER 27, 2000

JAGR STRETCHES HIS STREAK

COUNTLESS PENGUINS partisans will never forget the team's 5–0 victory against Toronto at Mellon Arena on this night, because it was when Mario Lemieux made his spectacular return from retirement after about three and a half years. Very few likely recall that Jaromir Jagr actually made a little history on Lemieux's first shift of the game. The opening period was just 33 seconds old when Jagr took a pass from Lemieux, who was below the Toronto goal line, and deposited a puck behind Maple Leafs goalie Curtis Joseph for the first of his two goals. That gave Jagr 20 or more goals in each of his 11 seasons with the Penguins, a streak that hasn't been matched by any Pittsburgh player, before or after him. Jagr actually scored 30 or more in 10 of those seasons—the only exception was his rookie year, 1990–91, when he had 27—which is another Pittsburgh record. When the air gets a bit more rarefied, however, Mario Lemieux is the one who has scrawled his name in the Penguins' record book, setting the marks for consecutive seasons with 40 goals (6) and 50 (3). Jagr had been widely acclaimed as the NHL's most gifted player after Lemieux retired, and Lemieux was impressed by what he saw of Jagr in their first game back together. "It was great to see," he said. "He was really into it from the start. We expect great things out of him. He's our leader, and he's the best player in the world."

Jaromir Jagr added to his long list of achievements on the night when Mario Lemieux got all the headlines.
COURTESY OF GETTY IMAGES

Jaromir Jagr and Mario Lemieux gave the Penguins a one-two punch with few equals in league history. COURTESY OF GETTY IMAGES

DECEMBER 30, 2000

LEMIEUX, JAGR HIT MILESTONES

IT TOOK Jaromir Jagr 763 games to rack up 1,000 points in the NHL. That's quite an accomplishment, but it doesn't really rival Mario Lemieux recording 1,500 in 747 games. Perhaps the most surprising thing was for them to hit these marks on the same night, as happened during a 5–3 victory against Ottawa at the Civic Arena. "That was something special for both of us, because we've played so many years together and accomplished so much," Lemieux said. He reached his milestone by scoring one goal and assisting on three others; Jagr scored two and set up one. Jagr reached four figures when he rapped a Lemieux rebound past Ottawa goalie Jani Hurme, and he insisted he was pleased that he didn't get to the milestone when Lemieux had come out of retirement a few nights earlier. "I wanted to make sure I didn't get [to] 1,000 in the last game," he said. "That would have meant nothing. This is a lot better."

Although Darius Kasparaitis wasn't much of a goal scorer, he got one when the Penguins needed it most. COURTESY OF GETTY IMAGES

MAY 10, 2001

KASPARAITIS CASHES IN

THE STANLEY CUP playoffs often create the most unlikely of heroes, and they don't get much more unlikely than Darius Kasparaitis. He was a fierce competitor known for delivering big hits and playing with a nasty edge any time he went over the boards. He was not known for his goal-scoring prowess. Not even a little. Which probably meant he was the obvious candidate to score the overtime goal that lifted the Penguins over Buffalo, 3–2, in Game 7 of their second-round series at HSBC Arena. "I haven't seen [Kasparaitis] score a goal in practice, never mind in a game," left winger Kevin Stevens said. "If I had to pick one guy, he'd be the least [likely] to score." Fair, on all counts, but none of that mattered when Kasparaitis joined a rush and took a pass from Robert Lang before throwing a shot past the glove of Sabres goalie Dominik Hasek to end the series. "We're here and we're celebrating, so it means somebody scored," Kasparaitis said. "Guys started hugging me, so it means I did it."

JULY 11, 2001

AND THEN HE WAS GONE

THERE WAS little doubt that Jaromir Jagr's run with the Penguins was coming to an end, because they simply didn't have the financial wherewithal to satisfy his contract demands and he had informed GM Craig Patrick two days after the season ended that he was interested in moving on. What wasn't clear was where he would end up, because a number of clubs expressed interest in acquiring him. Washington turned out to be the destination, as Patrick sent Jagr, whose extensive legacy in Pittsburgh included scoring 14 game-winning goals in 140 playoff appearances, and defenseman Frantisek Kucera to the Capitals for forwards Kris Beech and Michal Sivek and defenseman Ross Lupaschuk, three of Washington's most highly regarded prospects. "It's the highest-anxiety trade I've ever had to make," Patrick said. "There were a couple of others that were like that but they were a long time ago. This one was really difficult to deal with. All the emotions that are involved . . . all the things he's done here . . . it's sad that he wanted to leave." The deal proved to be the antithesis of one that works out well for both clubs. None of the players the Penguins received had a significant impact for them, and Jagr spent just three years in Washington before moving on to the New York Rangers.

Financial issues caused the Penguins to part ways with Jaromir Jagr after a spectacular 11-year run. COURTESY OF GETTY IMAGES

Craig Patrick decided Marc-Andre Fleury was a goalie around whom the Penguins could build.
COURTESY OF GETTY IMAGES

JUNE 21, 2003

THE FIRST BUILDING BLOCK

FEW LIKELY realized it at the time, but GM Craig Patrick took the first major step toward constructing the roster that would win Stanley Cups in 2009, 2016, and 2017 a few hours before the start of the NHL Draft in Nashville, as he traded the number three pick in the opening round, a second-round pick, and forward Mikael Samuelsson to Florida for the first choice in Round 1 as well as a third-rounder. The Panthers invested the first-rounder in forward Nathan Horton, whose career was cut short by injuries. Patrick, meanwhile, used the number one overall selection to claim goaltender Marc-Andre Fleury. "We're in a rebuilding mode—we've made that pretty clear—and we decided the best place to start building was in goal," Patrick said. Fleury would go on to become the most accomplished goalie in franchise history and, for that matter, one of the finest to grace the NHL. Before the Penguins sent him to Vegas in the 2017 expansion draft, Fleury was part of three Cup-winning clubs and set numerous team records. He also developed into one of the most popular players ever to pass through the franchise, beloved by both teammates and fans.

OCTOBER 10, 2003

LOCAL BOY MAKES GOOD

WESTERN PENNSYLVANIA was something of a hockey desert during the Penguins' early years in the NHL. The region had only a handful of indoor rinks, and few high schools sanctioned teams to compete against other districts, as was the norm in most other areas. But interest began to rise—and ultimately, spike—after Mario Lemieux joined the Penguins in 1984. More young athletes took up the game, and it was inevitable that some eventually would wear their hometown team's colors. And so it was that Pittsburgh invested its fourth-round pick in the 1999 draft in Ryan Malone, a winger and Upper St. Clair native. He made his NHL debut in a 3–0 loss to Los Angeles at Mellon Arena and, despite becoming the first-ever Western Pennsylvania native to play for the Penguins, was largely overshadowed that night, since rookie goalie Marc-Andre Fleury also made his NHL debut, and wowed the crowd with a 46-save performance that earned him recognition as the game's number one star. Although Malone's impact that night was limited—he played just 10:18 and was credited with one of the Penguins' 11 shots on goal—he would go on to accumulate 87 goals and 82 assists in 299 games before departing for Tampa Bay as a free agent in 2008, when he signed a seven-year, $31.5 million contract.

Western Pennsylvania native Ryan Malone developed into an impact player with his hometown team.
COURTESY OF GETTY IMAGES

APRIL 6, 2004

HOW TO WIN BY LOSING

THE 2003-04 SEASON was the latest in a series of forgettable ones for the Penguins, whose championship runs more than a decade earlier had become distant memories, and they sunk to the bottom of the overall standings. The only positive, it seemed, was that their 23–47–8–4 record put them in a favorable position to land the rights to Alex Ovechkin, a prolific goal-scorer from Russia. Ovechkin seemed like the kind of talent who not only could sell tickets but could be a foundation piece of the Penguins' ongoing rebuild. It turned out that Ovechkin would reach, and probably exceed, all expectations of how he would fare in the NHL. Unfortunately for the Penguins, he would do it for Washington, as the Capitals won the NHL draft lottery, moving from third to first in the order of selection. That bumped the Penguins down to the second pick in Round 1, but they ended up with a pretty fair consolation prize: Russian center Evgeni Malkin, who eventually would team up with Sidney Crosby to give Pittsburgh an exceptional tandem at that position for the better part of two decades. Along the way, Malkin would collect rookie of the year honors, two scoring titles, an MVP award, and a playoff MVP award to go with three Stanley Cups.

The Penguins lost the draft lottery in 2004, dropping to second in the order of selection, but they still landed Evgeni Malkin.
COURTESY OF GETTY IMAGES

JUNE 9, 2004

COFFEY, MURPHY NAMED TO HALL OF FAME

IN SOME WAYS, Paul Coffey and Larry Murphy could not have been more different, and not only because Coffey was a left-handed shot and Murphy was a righty. Coffey was a breathtaking skater, one with few, if any, equals in NHL history, and his speed complemented an outstanding skills set. He was quite capable of making things exciting at both ends of the ice. Conversely, Murphy rarely, if ever, did anything spectacular, playing a solid, reliable style all over the ice. Still, they did have a few things in common. Both played for the Penguins' Stanley Cup–winning team in 1991 and retired with four championship rings. Both played for the same youth team in suburban Toronto. And both were so accomplished at their jobs that they were selected for induction to the Hockey Hall of Fame. "To have two guys from the same minor hockey team win the Stanley Cup together and go into the Hall of Fame together . . . statistically, that's just incredible," Murphy said. Oh, and they shared at least one more thing: their reaction to getting the call that they'd be entering the Hall with Raymond Bourque and Cliff Fletcher. "When you get a call like that, you're just blown away by it," Coffey said. Murphy certainly was. "It hit me harder than I anticipated," he said. "I was almost not prepared for how excited I was."

Paul Coffey and Larry Murphy earned Stanley Cup rings with the Penguins in 1991, and Hall of Fame rings when their careers were over.
COURTESY OF GETTY IMAGES

One of the most important victories in Penguins history happened off the ice in 2005.
COURTESY OF GETTY IMAGES

JULY 22, 2005

NOW THAT'S WINNING A LOTTERY

THE 2004-05 NHL season was wiped out by a labor dispute, so the league adopted a weighted lottery to determine the order of selection for the 2005 draft. The Penguins went in as one of four teams with the best odds of landing the top pick, but like Buffalo, Columbus, and the New York Rangers, they had just a 6.3 percent chance of securing it. But as the lottery progressed, the Penguins remained in contention. Finally, the field had been trimmed to two teams, Anaheim and the Penguins. On the line were the rights to a player regarded as the game's most promising prospect in decades, a guy who had the potential to lead his team to multiple championships because of his extraordinary blend of talent and tenacity: a center named Sidney Crosby from Rimouski of the Quebec Major Junior Hockey League. "People have said he's got the vision of a Wayne Gretzky and the goal-scoring and playmaking ability of Mario Lemieux," GM Craig Patrick said. Although Patrick's team had had more than its share of tough luck over the years, particularly during the franchise's first 15 or so seasons, a lot of that misfortune was wiped out in an instant, as they, not the Mighty Ducks, ended up with the top pick in the draft, which was conducted eight days later at a hotel in Ottawa. "It's a very, very lucky day," Patrick said. "It's about time."

OCTOBER 5, 2005

OFF TO A SLOW START

SIDNEY CROSBY made his NHL debut at Continental Airlines Arena in East Rutherford, New Jersey, but there wasn't much memorable about it, for him or his team. Crosby recorded his first professional point, an assist on Mark Recchi's power-play goal in the third period, but the Penguins were soundly defeated by the New Jersey Devils, 5–1. The crowd rubbed it in by chanting "Parise's better" at Crosby, and while that assessment of Zach Parise's abilities compared to those of Crosby would not hold up over time, it had to sting Crosby a bit at the moment. Crosby allowed after his first pro game that, "You might get caught watching a little bit," and while his performance against the Devils was nothing special, New Jersey coach Larry Robinson, a Hall of Fame defenseman, said he was confident Crosby could live up to the great expectations so many had for him. "There was only one Gordie Howe, one Jean Beliveau, and there is only one Mario Lemieux," Robinson said. "This kid has a big weight to bear and a big burden. Hopefully, he'll be able to handle it. I think he can."

Unlike so much of what followed it, there was little to remember about Sidney Crosby's NHL debut. COURTESY OF GETTY IMAGES

Mario Lemieux, the heart of the team for so many years, had to retire for good because of an irregular heartbeat. COURTESY OF GETTY IMAGES

DECEMBER 16, 2005

THIS TIME, FOR SURE

MARIO LEMIEUX appeared in his 915th—and what proved to be his final—NHL game, a 4–3 overtime loss at home to the Buffalo Sabres. His career finale wasn't nearly as spectacular as his NHL debut in 1984 had been, as Lemieux was credited with only one assist and one shot on goal, but it was not clear at the time that his playing days had come to an end, because Lemieux did not formally announce that he was giving up the game until January 24, 2006. His second (and permanent) departure from active duty was necessitated not because of the health issues that had dogged him earlier in his career, including cancer and recurring back problems, but because of atrial fibrillation (an irregular heartbeat). Lemieux would remain in his role as owner for another 16 years and remains the most popular and important figure in franchise history, on and off the ice. Ironically, hours before the Buffalo game, rookie Sidney Crosby, who was Lemieux's heir apparent as the face of the franchise, was named an alternate captain by coach Michel Therrien. It was a rare honor for a first-year player, and one Lemieux was quick to endorse. "They told me he was getting the [captaincy]," Lemieux said, smiling. Crosby actually did succeed Lemieux as captain, although he didn't get the "C" until 2007, and that clearly is what Therrien was preparing him for. "I want him to learn," Therrien said. "Because eventually, it's going to be Sidney's team."

APRIL 17, 2006

NO TIME TO WASTE

IT DIDN'T take long for most folks to realize that Sidney Crosby was capable of meeting, if not exceeding, even the most grandiose expectations of the impact he could have in the NHL. But any remaining doubters likely were convinced when he set up a Ryan Malone goal—his third assist in a 6–1 victory over the New York Islanders at Mellon Arena—to become the youngest player in NHL history to reach 100 points. He was 18 years and 253 days old when he reached that milestone; the previous record-holder, Dale Hawerchuk of Winnipeg, was 18 years, 354 days old when he did it. "It's nice to get [100]," Crosby said. "It's nice to have the weight off your shoulders." He got point number 100 on a fairly ordinary 15-foot forehand pass to Ryan Malone, who buried a shot past New York goalie Garth Snow, but Crosby insisted he didn't care that it wasn't one of his more breathtaking setups. "I'm not going to complain," he said. "If it would have been an empty-net [goal], I wouldn't have complained. Malone certainly wasn't, since he figured in this slice of hockey history. "It's a story to tell my friends, sitting at the bar this summer," he said. "And something to tell my kids."

Sidney Crosby scrawled his signature in the NHL record book for the first time near the end of his rookie season. COURTESY OF GETTY IMAGES

MAY 25, 2006

PATRICK OUT, SHERO IN

CRAIG PATRICK, arguably the best general manager the Penguins have had, was replaced as GM by Ray Shero, son of former NHL coach Fred Shero. Patrick had assembled the Penguins' first Cup-winning teams and remained a shrewd evaluator of talent, but ownership decided the team needed to modernize the GM's approach to overseeing the organization and had fired him about a month earlier. Shero joined the Penguins with experience as a player agent and was coming off a successful stint as David Poile's assistant GM in Nashville. Although history would show that the Penguins went a long way toward prepping for their second batch of Cups while Patrick was in charge—he, after all, is the GM who traded for the right to draft Marc-Andre Fleury and drafted Sidney Crosby and Evgeni Malkin, although neither of those picks qualified as anything close to a reach—Shero would pull off some shrewd personnel moves, like adding wingers Bill Guerin and Chris Kunitz, that made the Penguins' third title possible in 2009. The day he was hired, Shero was adamant that he would make whatever personnel changes he deemed necessary to restore Pittsburgh to its status as a perennial contender. "There are all different ways to build this team," he said. "We have to look at all of them."

Ownership sought to rejuvenate the franchise by hiring Ray Shero to replace Craig Patrick as GM. COURTESY OF GETTY IMAGES

OCTOBER 12, 2006

JORDAN STAAL STARTS STRONG

JUST MONTHS after the Penguins drafted him with the obvious intent of having him provide a strong defensive presence on the third line, Jordan Staal opened the scoring in a 6–5 victory over the New York Rangers at Madison Square Garden with an unassisted, shorthanded goal. In the process, Staal, who was 32 days past his 18th birthday, became the 10th-youngest player in NHL history to score a goal. Staal earned that footnote in league history by stealing the puck in the Penguins' zone, nudging it into the neutral zone, and then outracing New York defenseman Michal Rozsival before launching a shot past Rangers goalie Henrik Lundqvist at 3:23 of the opening period. "My mind kind of went blank, and I just kind of went with it," Staal said. "And it worked out." So did most of his time with the Penguins, and Staal would make it into the league record book again before his first season was over. On February 10, 2007, he became the youngest player in the league to record a hat trick, racking up three goals during a 6–5 victory in Toronto when he was 18 years, 153 days old. That was 23 days younger than Toronto's Jack Hamilton was when he put in four against the New York Rangers on December 4, 1943.

Jordan Staal gave the Penguins a strong number three center behind Sidney Crosby and Evgeni Malkin. COURTESY OF GETTY IMAGES

NOVEMBER 1, 2006

MALKIN MAKES MAGIC

EVGENI MALKIN put up a pair of goals, including the overtime winner, in a 4–3 victory at Los Angeles to become the first NHL player in 89 years to score in each of his first six games in the league. He did it in style, recording his first goal during the opening period and then getting the game winner at 2:45 of overtime. The select company Malkin joined includes three players, all of whom managed that feat during the 1917–18 season, which just happened to be the NHL's first in operation. Members of that trio were Joe Malone, Cy Denneny, and Newsy Lalonde. If his early-season rampage didn't sufficiently establish Malkin's offensive credentials at the pro level—and they certainly should have—he burnished them again on January 20, 2007, when he had five assists in an 8–2 win over the Toronto Maple Leafs at Mellon Arena to join Mario Lemieux as the only Penguins rookies to get five or more points in a game. Those feats were part of the reason Malkin would receive the Calder Trophy as the NHL's top rookie.

Evgeni Malkin didn't exactly slip onto the scene quietly once he made it to the NHL. COURTESY OF GETTY IMAGES

Making it through the season without losing a game to Philadelphia was a cause for celebration.
COURTESY OF GETTY IMAGES

MARCH 4, 2007

HOW SWEEP IT IS

PHILADELPHIA TORMENTED the Penguins for most of their first quarter century of existence, so longtime Penguins partisans surely took extra delight when their team defeated the Flyers, 4–3, in a shoot-out at Mellon Arena to record their eighth victory in the eight-game season series. It marked the first time the Penguins defeated an opponent eight times in a season, surpassing the previous mark of six that had been set against Boston (1993–94), Ottawa (1995–96), and Carolina (1997–98). Whether the Penguins truly pulled off a sweep was a matter of perspective, since losing in overtime twice allowed the Flyers to take a pair of points out of the season series, but Pittsburgh was more focused on avoiding future repeats of a dismal first period that almost rendered the sweep discussions moot. Coach Michel Therrien said his team's play during those 20 minutes "looked like a nightmare," and that might have been understating it. "We could have played a lot better," defenseman Ryan Whitney said. The *Post-Gazette*'s game story agreed, adding that would have been true "even if they had been wearing blindfolds and street shoes." They did manage to overcome the miserable start, however, and rack up their eighth win in eight tries against their most bitter rival. "We found a way," winger Gary Roberts said. "And that's the big thing."

MARCH 13, 2007

ARENA DEAL FINALLY DONE

MARIO LEMIEUX was able to do some incredible things in milliseconds during his playing days, but getting things done as an owner took a lot more time. That certainly was true of working out a deal for a new venue to replace Mellon Arena; it wasn't struck until eight years after Lemieux had taken ownership of the franchise. The price tag for the building was $290 million and included a guarantee that the Penguins would remain in Pittsburgh for at least 30 years. That latter was quite significant, since Lemieux and his co-owner, Ron Burkle, had floated the threat of relocating the team little more than a week earlier. "I've said many times that my goal was to keep the Penguins here forever and eventually win the Stanley Cup," Lemieux said. "We have one out of the two. It's a good start." Governor Ed Rendell noted that Lemieux and Burkle had turned down a proposal to move to Kansas City, offering no rent or construction costs and 75 percent of the revenues at the newly built Sprint Center. "Kansas City and other cities might have given the Penguins better financial deals," he said. "But no one could guarantee the Penguins the strength, the loyalty, and support Pittsburgh fans have offered them over the years."

Finalizing an agreement for a new arena was key to securing the Penguins' long-term future in Pittsburgh.
PUBLIC DOMAIN

Sidney Crosby needed just two seasons to become the highest-scoring player in the NHL.
COURTESY OF GETTY IMAGES

APRIL 7, 2007

CROSBY'S FEATS NEVER GET OLD

O ***THE PENGUINS'*** regular-season finale, a 2–1 win against the New York Rangers at Mellon Arena, was bittersweet. They weren't able to secure home-ice advantage for the first-round playoff series against Ottawa—the Penguins' first postseason action since 2001—because the Senators were 6–3 victors in Boston that night. On the other hand, Sidney Crosby was able to lock up yet another entry in the NHL record book by becoming the youngest player to win an Art Ross Trophy as the league's top scorer. He swelled his points total for the season to 120, six more than the runner-up, San Jose center Joe Thornton. "It's a nice accomplishment," said Crosby, 19. "I didn't come into this season expecting it. I just tried to have the best season possible, and was lucky enough to get it." Crosby, who finished with 36 goals and 84 assists, was the youngest player to win a scoring title in any of the major North American sports, and continues to hold that distinction in the NHL.

MAY 31, 2007

CAN'T SPELL CROSBY WITHOUT A "C"

SIDNEY CROSBY accomplished an awful lot of things during his first two seasons in the NHL. One of them was convincing management to make him the youngest captain the NHL had ever seen. Actually, it was more a case of his bosses convincing Crosby to take on that role, since he previously had rebuffed efforts by coach Michel Therrien and GM Ray Shero to assume that role. "When it was brought up [by Shero] in January, I had a little doubt, and you have to be into it all the way," Crosby said. "You have to be ready for the responsibility, and I've accepted that." The team had not had a captain since Mario Lemieux retired in 2006, and Crosby had been serving as one of its three alternate captains. "He's ready for it," Therrien said. "You want to have guys like that to lead your team. I knew when I gave him the 'A' that when it was the right time, he was going to be ready" for the captaincy. And that time had arrived. "I was always told that age is just a number," Crosby said. "And I try to not let it get in the way of anything."

Making Sidney Crosby the youngest captain in NHL history formalized his status as the Penguins' leader.
COURTESY OF GETTY IMAGES

Future Hall of Famer Mark Recchi's second stint with the Penguins came to a disappointing end.
COURTESY OF GETTY IMAGES

DECEMBER 8, 2008

RECCHI HEADS SOUTH

MARK RECCHI was extremely popular and productive after he broke into the NHL with the Penguins during the 1988–89 season and ended up returning to Pittsburgh for a couple of more stints while overachieving his way into the Hockey Hall of Fame. His ties to the franchise—as a player, anyway—finally were severed for good when he was claimed off reentry waivers by the Atlanta Thrashers. (Had Atlanta, or any other team, grabbed him when he was on conventional waivers a day earlier, that club would have been responsible for his entire, prorated $1.75 million salary. Because he was taken off reentry waivers, the Penguins had to pick up half of that.) The Penguins were in the midst of a youth movement when Recchi was waived and, at age 39, it was clear he did not have a place in their future. "The end result was good for both," GM Ray Shero said. "And I hope it's a real good fit for him." Some teammates left no doubt that they were sorry to see him go. "We're all very happy for him, that he's getting an opportunity to play," winger Gary Roberts said. "We know he can still play and wants to play. He left his mark here."

Sidney Crosby made sure the NHL's initial Winter Classic was worthy of the name.
COURTESY OF GETTY IMAGES

JANUARY 1, 2008

AN INSTANT CLASSIC

NO ONE was certain what to expect when the NHL scheduled its first Winter Classic game for Ralph Wilson Stadium in Orchard Park, New York. What the league got couldn't have been scripted any better. The crowd of 71,217 was larger than any that ever had seen an NHL game. The weather conditions made it look at times as if the game were being played inside a snow globe, and—perhaps best of all, from a public-exposure perspective—Sidney Crosby scored the shoot-out-deciding goal in Pittsburgh's 2–1 win. "Especially with Sid getting the winner, I thought it was a good ending," Penguins winger Colby Armstrong said. Crosby ended the game when, with the shoot-out tied, 1–1, he tossed a puck between the legs of Sabres goalie Ryan Miller. "It couldn't have worked out better for [NBC]," Pittsburgh defenseman Ryan Whitney said. "They got the snowfall. They got Sidney to end the game. That's just what they wanted."

JUNE 2, 2008

SYKORA KEEPS THE SEASON GOING

THE PENGUINS were one goal away from elimination when Game 5 of the Stanley Cup Final at Joe Louis Arena in Detroit went to overtime. The same was true when the first 20 minutes passed. And again following the second extra period. But Penguins winger Petr Sykora guaranteed there would be no fourth overtime—and that there would be a Game 6—when he beat Red Wings goalie Chris Osgood from the right dot midway through the third OT for a 4–3 victory and one of the most dramatic wins in franchise history. "I hated to see Petr Sykora get that puck," Detroit coach Mike Babcock said. "You just know it's going in." The Red Wings had come within 34.3 seconds of taking the Cup in regulation, but Max Talbot kept the game going after going on the ice as the extra attacker after goalie Marc-Andre Fleury had been pulled—the first time Talbot filled that role during the 2007–08 season. "[Coach Michel Therrien] had a feeling, and he went with it," Talbot said. "I was in the right place at the right moment, and the puck was in the back of the net." And the series was headed back to Pittsburgh.

Petr Sykora wouldn't let the Penguins' bid for a Stanley Cup end in five games. COURTESY OF GETTY IMAGES

JUNE 4, 2008

A REAL HEARTBREAKER

THE PENGUINS were not necessarily a popular choice to reach the Stanley Cup Final, and might have overachieved to get there. That didn't make it any easier to accept it when their bid for a championship ended, however. Detroit beat them 3–2 in Game 6 of the Cup Final at Mellon Arena after

The Penguins' spirited run at the team's third Cup came up just a bit short in a six-game loss to Detroit. COURTESY OF GETTY IMAGES

the Penguins came within a few millimeters of forcing overtime as the third period was winding down. "It was really close," said Red Wings winger Mikael Samuelsson, a former Penguin whose old team clearly was gutted by the way its season ended. "I'm almost speechless right now," coach Michel Therrien said. "When you're that close, it is really tough. . . . The hockey gods were not on our side tonight. It hurts. You could feel the pain." Owner Mario Lemieux certainly did, but he also saw the potential of the group that had been assembled. "We've come a long way in a short period of time," he said. "It's going to be a great team for many years to come."

With the Penguins sputtering, Ray Shero fired Michel Therrien as coach and brought in Dan Bylsma to succeed him. COURTESY OF GETTY IMAGES

FEBRUARY 15, 2009

DAN BYLSMA ENTERS

THE PENGUINS, who had come within two wins of capturing the Stanley Cup in the spring of 2008, were in danger of sitting out the playoffs as the stretch drive loomed. That prompted GM Ray Shero to replace coach Michel Therrien with Dan Bylsma, officially on an interim basis. "I didn't like the direction in which the team was headed," Shero said. The change came a day after the Penguins had taken a 2–0 lead in Toronto and then yielded six unanswered goals. "It wasn't so much the outcome," Shero said. "It was how the game was played that I was disappointed in." He described Bylsma as "one of the up-and-coming coaches" in the sport. Bylsma, a blue-collar winger during his playing days, had been coaching the Penguins' farm team in Wilkes-Barre. Bylsma had a clear strategy for the approach he planned to take behind the Penguins' bench. "We need to force teams to deal with the quality of players we have at every position," he said. "To get the opportunity to coach a team with this much talent and this much possibility, it's a great thing. It's a great chance for me." The Penguins finished the season with an 18–3–4 record under Bylsma.

MARCH 8, 2009

AT HOME ON THE ROAD

THE PENGUINS were on a positive roll after Dan Bylsma succeeded Michel Therrien as coach, and they were confident they could do just about anything. Even so, none of them predicted that they would be the first club in franchise history to win every game on a five-game road trip, but they did just that after a 4–3 shoot-out victory in the trip finale at the Verizon Center in Washington. "Everybody was confident," goalie Marc-Andre Fleury said. "But expecting 5–0 would have been pushing it a little bit." The victory over the Capitals completed a trip that included wins at Chicago, Dallas, Tampa, and Florida. Sidney Crosby, the target of considerable crowd abuse when the Penguins played in Washington, scored their first goal and then sealed the victory by being the only shooter on either side to succeed in the shoot-out. Fleury did his part by thwarting all three of the skilled Washington forwards—Alexander Semin, Viktor Kozlov, and Alex Ovechkin—he faced in the shoot-out. "I knew they had some good shooters," he said. "That makes it more fun to win it."

Venturing outside of Pittsburgh wasn't a problem for the Penguins as the 2008-09 season wound down.
COURTESY OF GETTY IMAGES

Max Talbot turned the series-clinching game against Philadelphia in the Penguins' favor by getting beaten up. COURTESY OF GETTY IMAGES

APRIL 25, 2009

TAKING ONE FOR THE TEAM

MAX TALBOT checked in at 5-foot-11, 186 pounds, and whether those vital stats were recorded while he was wearing skates and had stuffed his pockets with pucks might never be known. Regardless, no one ever suggested that he got into the game to be an enforcer. But when the Penguins needed it most, in the second period of Game 6 of their first-round playoff series with Philadelphia, Talbot stepped up and traded punches with Flyers tough guy Daniel Carcillo. And got a sound beating for his trouble. That seemed like another unpleasant footnote in a miserable afternoon for the Penguins, but it proved to be a turning point. Fourteen seconds after the fight, Ruslan Fedetenko scored to slice Philadelphia's lead at the Wachovia Center to 3–1—and trigger a run of five unanswered goals for the Penguins to move them into Round 2. And while Talbot wasn't cited as one of the game's three stars, his teammates pointed to him as the pivotal figure in the game. "Max really stepped up," winger Tyler Kennedy said. "He showed a ton of guts." A Talbot turnover had led to Philadelphia's first goal, and he said fighting Carcillo was part of the way he tried to atone for it. "I had to make up for that," he said. "That seemed like a good way to do it."

MAY 4, 2009

TIP OF THE HATS FOR TWO GREATS

O**SIDNEY CROSBY** and Washington's Alex Ovechkin had emerged as the faces of the NHL long before their clubs met in Round 2 of the 2009 playoffs, and both showed in that series that they were worthy of all the attention. That was especially true in the Capitals' 4–3 victory in Game 2, when Ovechkin led his team by scoring three goals while Crosby recorded a hat trick of his own for the Penguins. "This is everything the media made it out to be," Washington defenseman Mike Green said. "It's a battle of the two best players in hockey and tonight, they both carried their teams." Penguins coach Dan Bylsma suggested that "They apparently heard the hype and are living up to it," while his Capitals counterpart said, "It's great for our sport. That's why they are who they are. Not too many people can do what they did tonight." But for one of those people, there wasn't much solace in his individual achievement. "It's nice scoring goals," Crosby said. "But I'd rather win."

Sidney Crosby and Alex Ovechkin put on a show in Game 2 of the Penguins' Round 2 series with Washington. COURTESY OF GETTY IMAGES

MAY 13, 2009

FLEURY ROBS OVECHKIN

MARC-ANDRE FLEURY made 3,002 saves in 115 playoff appearances during his time with the Penguins, but two of his most famous came just weeks apart. The first came in Game 7 of their second-round playoff series with Washington, when Fleury used his glove to deny Capitals winger Alex Ovechkin on a breakaway in the early minutes of what would become a 6–2 Penguins win at the Verizon Center that hoisted them into the Eastern Conference Final against Carolina. Fleury's sequel would come in the Stanley Cup Final against Detroit, but the Penguins might never have made it to Round 2 if Fleury hadn't robbed Ovechkin when he broke in alone with the score tied, 0–0. "If that goes in, who knows where the game goes?" Pittsburgh defenseman Brooks Orpik said. "I was thinking to myself right after that, 'Maybe that's the turning point in the game.' It's definitely something you look back on. After that, we kind of dictated the play." And kept playing for three more rounds.

Marc-Andre Fleury's remarkable glove save on an Alex Ovechkin breakaway set the tone for Game 7.
COURTESY OF GETTY IMAGES

Max Talbot was unlikely to be the offensive hero of a Cup-deciding game . . . but he was all of that. COURTESY OF GETTY IMAGES

JUNE 12, 2009

IT'S TALBOT TIME

MAX TALBOT had figured prominently in the Penguins' postseason with his momentum-altering fight against Philadelphia's Daniel Carcillo during the opening round, but his role in Game 7 of the Stanley Cup Final at Joe Louis Arena in Detroit eclipsed anything Talbot—or most of his teammates—had done to that point of the playoffs. He scored both of the Penguins' goals in the 2–1 victory that gave the franchise its third Cup. "It's the biggest day of my life," Talbot said. "I'm not really thinking I'm a hero. I scored two goals, but everybody on this team is a hero. I wasn't trying to do anything special. I just wanted to win a Cup." And so he did, in part because goalie Marc-Andre Fleury, whose big-game credentials had been questioned since his junior hockey days, rejected 23 of 24 Detroit shots, including a lunging stop on defenseman Nicklas Lidstrom as time was about to expire in the third period. "I saw the shot coming in," Fleury said. "And I just tried to do everything I could to get over there." He made it, and a second later, the air in Joe Louis was filled with sticks, gloves, and howls of delight as Fleury and his teammates celebrated their championship. "It's everything you dream of," captain Sidney Crosby said. "It's an amazing feeling." The Penguins played more than half of Game 7 without Crosby, whose left knee was pinned to the boards at center ice on a hit from Detroit's Johan Franzen in the sixth minute of the second period. Crosby subsequently played just one 32-second shift, in the middle of the third period. "We tried to make it so I couldn't feel it anymore," Crosby said. "But it just didn't work." Turned out that the Penguins were able to get by without him, and the good news for them didn't end there, because Crosby pronounced himself to be "100 percent" for the Stanley Cup parade in Pittsburgh a few days later.

Sidney Crosby added a share of the 2009-10 Rocket Richard Trophy to his growing collection of NHL awards.
COURTESY OF GETTY IMAGES

APRIL 11, 2010

CROSBY WINS ROCKET RICHARD

ALTHOUGH SIDNEY CROSBY'S playmaking overshadowed his goal scoring throughout his career, he was able to find the net on a regular basis from the time he entered the NHL. He did it so often during the 2009–10 season that he earned a share of the Rocket Richard Trophy, awarded annually to the NHL's top goal producer. Crosby had two goals in the Penguins' regular-season finale, a 6–5 overtime victory over the New York Islanders at Nassau Coliseum, to swell his total to 51, and he came within seconds—literally—of having the Richard to himself. However, Tampa Bay's Steven Stamkos forced Crosby to share it with him by scoring with 13 seconds to play in a Lightning victory against Florida. "I was never one for ties, but I'll accept a tie, I guess," Crosby said. "It's not easy to score in this league, at all. Steven had a great season." Because the Tampa Bay–Florida game was contested a bit earlier than the one on Long Island, the Penguins knew Crosby needed to get a third goal to pass Stamkos, and coach Dan Bylsma acknowledged that "we were definitely trying to get him in a situation where he'd be able to try to get that goal."

The Penguins' long run at their original home rink ended with a disappointing defeat.
COURTESY OF GETTY IMAGES

MAY 12, 2010

END OF AN ERA

THE CURTAIN FELL on the Penguins' original home—the building known first as the Civic Arena, and later Mellon Arena—in a 5–2 loss to Montreal in Game 7 of a second-round playoff series in which the Canadiens upset the Penguins in large part because of the inspired play of goaltender Jaroslav Halak and the relentless goal-scoring of Michael Cammalleri. Game 7 started badly for Pittsburgh—the Penguins were assessed two penalties during the first 32 seconds of the opening period, with the first of those leading to Montreal's first goal—and never really got much better. "As a coach, you plan for different scenarios," coach Dan Bylsma said. "You can safely say this is one I didn't plan for." Jordan Staal would score the Penguins' final goal in the building during the second period of the series finale, while Montreal winger Brian Gionta would get the last one by a member of either team. Coincidentally enough, the Canadiens had defeated the Penguins, 2–1, in the first regular-season game at the arena.

OCTOBER 7, 2010

MOVING INTO A NEW HOME

O**MANY YEARS** and many disappointments after the process of trying to arrange for a building to replace the Civic Arena began, the Penguins moved into their new multipurpose home, across Centre Avenue from their old one. While their first regular-season game there produced a disappointing result—a 3–2 loss to archrival Philadelphia—the occasion was marked with a ceremony worthy of it. The highlight came when team co-owner Mario Lemieux stood at center ice brandishing a bottle filled with melted ice from the Civic Arena, the contents of which he poured onto the playing surface in his club's new venue, symbolically bonding the franchise's two eras to a roaring ovation from the crowd of 18,289, larger than any that had witnessed a hockey game in the city. NHL Commissoner Gary Bettman was present for the arena opening, and he credited the franchise's owners for making it possible. "You need to give Mario Lemieux and Ron Burkle credit for standing by their team and having the wisdom to know what could be there at the end," he said. "It's a testament to them. They believed in this franchise. We always knew Pittsburgh was a hockey town."

Mario Lemieux brought some melted ice from Mellon Arena to christen the playing surface at Consol Energy Center.
COURTESY OF GETTY IMAGES

JANUARY 1, 2011

A COSTLY CLASSIC

THE PENGUINS and Washington Capitals were supposed to meet in the NHL's annual Winter Classic game during the afternoon at Heinz Field, home of the NFL's Pittsburgh Steelers, but the game had to be pushed back to the evening because of heavy rains moving through Western Pennsylvania during the day. Too bad for the Penguins that it wasn't simply rained out. Losing to the Capitals 3–1 was bad enough, but infinitely worse for the Penguins was that Sidney Crosby was knocked out of the game after taking a blow to the head from Capitals forward David Steckel in the waning seconds of the second period. Crosby was in obvious discomfort after the hit, but was able to play in the third period and speak with reporters afterward. "I couldn't even tell you what happened," he said. "The puck was going the other way, and I turned. Next thing I know, I'm down. . . . It was pretty far behind the play, so maybe the refs didn't even see it." Steckel was not penalized on the play and insisted that "obviously, it wasn't intentional." Crosby was back in the lineup against Tampa Bay four nights later but left the game after Lightning defenseman Victor Hedman checked him into the boards and glass. Coach Dan Bylsma said Crosby had a "mild concussion" that was "not connected" to the blow delivered by Steckel. The initial prognosis was that Crosby would be sidelined about a week, but he wouldn't play again until late November.

The Penguins' loss to Washington in the 2011 Winter Classic cost them more than two points in the standings. COURTESY OF GETTY IMAGES

Sidney Crosby returned from his lengthy absence with an impact worthy of Mario Lemieux.
COURTESY OF GETTY IMAGES

NOVEMBER 21, 2011

AN EPIC CROSBY COMEBACK

SIDNEY CROSBY hadn't appeared in a game in about 10½ months while recovering from a severe concussion, so it was only fair that expectations for his play when he returned to the lineup were tempered. Fair, but not necessary, because Crosby scored two goals and assisted on two others in a 5–0 victory against the New York Islanders at Consol Energy Center. "I've been waiting a long time to have this chance to go out there," he said. "I wanted to make sure I gave it my best effort." Suffice it to say, the guys with whom he shared a locker room figured he did all of that. And a lot more. "Some of the plays, the way he played . . . there's a lot of things that were special," coach Dan Bylsma said. Teammate Zbynek Michalek offered a simple assessment that had to be chilling to the rest of the league—"He's going to get even better."—but Crosby was focused mainly on just being back at work. "The goals and assists were great, obviously," he said. "But just being back out there, I can't really describe it. The main thing was just the joy of playing."

JUNE 22, 2012

OH, BROTHER. STAAL TACTICS FORCE A DEAL

THE PENGUINS played host to the NHL Draft for the second time—they'd done it at their previous home on the other side of Centre Avenue in 1997—and made sure they did it with a splash. After failing to convince Jordan Staal to accept a 10-year contract reportedly worth $6 million per season, GM Ray Shero honored Staal's request to trade him to Carolina, where he would be reunited with his brother Eric, and got a first-round draft choice, center Brandon Sutter, and defense prospect Brian Dumoulin in return. Shero used the first-rounder on defenseman Derrick Pouliot, who never lived up to expectations, but Sutter proved to be an effective replacement for Staal in the middle of the third line and Dumoulin was a stalwart on the Penguins' blue line for a decade. "It certainly was a fair hockey trade," said Hurricanes GM Jim Rutherford, who noted that working out the deal took about two and a half hours on the day it was consummated.

Jordan Staal wanted the Penguins to trade him to Carolina so he could play alongside his older brother, Eric. COURTESY OF GETTY IMAGES

Jarome Iginla was a go-for-broke addition by Ray Shero at the NHL trade deadline.
COURTESY OF GETTY IMAGES

MARCH 27, 2013

RAY SHERO GOES FOR BROKE

O**GM RAY SHERO** didn't just reinforce the Penguins' lineup for a playoff run as the 2013 NHL trade deadline approached. He moved aggressively to construct a roster that entered the postseason as a popular choice to win another championship. The coup de grace came when he acquired Hall-of-Famer-in-waiting Jarome Iginla from Calgary to add another dimension to an already-imposing collection of forwards, a move that came after he had brought in forward Brenden Morrow, whose game was an impressive hybrid of talent and intangibles, and rugged defenseman Douglas Murray of San Jose. "We're all in," Shero said. "We want to win." Those additions came while the Penguins were accumulating 15 consecutive victories, tying the second-longest such streak in NHL history. Things soured almost immediately, however, as Sidney Crosby had his jaw broken when he was struck in the face by a shot from teammate Brooks Orpik. Crosby had to undergo oral surgery to repair damage done to his teeth and had to sit out the rest of the regular season and the first game of the playoffs. The Penguins managed to win their first two rounds, against the New York Islanders and Ottawa, but were swept by Boston in the Eastern Conference Final, when their ultrapotent offense was able to generate just two goals in four games.

JUNE 6, 2014

JIM RUTHERFORD RETURNS

O**ANOTHER DISAPPOINTING** playoff performance—the Penguins lost the final three games of their second-round series against the New York Rangers after getting by Columbus in Round 1—cost GM Ray Shero and coach Dan Bylsma their jobs, and the Penguins went deep into their history to find Shero's replacement. They settled on Jim Rutherford, a longtime GM and executive with Carolina who had been a goaltender with the Penguins in the early 1970s. While Rutherford's work in the Pittsburgh net hadn't been anything special—he was 44–49 with 14 ties in 115 regular-season appearances—he would go on to enhance what would become a Hall of Fame résumé, orchestrating personnel moves that would help to make the Penguins' Stanley Cup triumphs in 2016 and 2017 possible. Although his first choice as coach, Mike Johnston, produced pedestrian results during his time behind the bench, Rutherford struck it rich with his second, Mike Sullivan. Rutherford initially selected him in 2015 to coach the Penguins' American Hockey League affiliate in Wilkes-Barre, but promoted him to the parent club a few months later, on December 12. The Penguins were celebrating Cup number four the following spring.

New GM Jim Rutherford (right) remade the coaching staff by bringing in assistant Rick Tocchet and head coach Mike Johnston. COURTESY OF GETTY IMAGES

Gritty winger Patric Hornqvist proved to be a valuable addition when he was acquired from Nashville. COURTESY OF GETTY IMAGES

JUNE 27, 2014

PATRIC HORNQVIST COMES ABOARD

JIM RUTHERFORD didn't wait long to begin putting his mark on the Penguins' roster, as he sent high-scoring winger James Neal to Nashville for gritty winger Patric Hornqvist and defensive forward Nick Spaling just three weeks after taking over as GM. Hornqvist had been the final player selected in the 2005 NHL Draft, in which Sidney Crosby had gone first overall. Rutherford, who said about 15 clubs had expressed interest in acquiring Neal, was drawn to Hornqvist because of his willingness to operate in high-traffic areas around the net and his knack for annoying opponents, often getting them to focus more on trying to punish him than on their on-ice responsibilities. Rutherford also suggested that, in addition to his on-ice contributions, he could provide a badly needed ingredient to the team's chemistry. "Hornqvist plays with an edge," he said. "Goes to the net. Works the corners. . . . We were just trying to change the [personnel] mix of our team a little bit and get a little bit different type player."

JULY 1, 2015

RUTHERFORD PULLS A STUNNER

PHIL KESSEL is among the most enigmatic players to pass through the NHL in recent seasons, but Jim Rutherford and his staff determined that he could be a valuable addition to the Penguins' roster, so Rutherford negotiated a multifaceted trade to bring him in from Toronto. Rutherford sent the Maple Leafs first- and third-round draft choices in 2016, forwards Kasperi Kapanen and Nick Spaling, and defenseman Scott Harrington for Kessel, defenseman Tim Erixon, forward Tyler Biggs, and a conditional second-round draft choice. Kessel easily was the biggest name in that swap, and he proved to be the one who had the biggest impact, too. He was a key member of the Penguins' Cup-winning clubs in 2016 and 2017, as he manufactured 18 goals and 27 assists in 49 playoff games during those two title runs. Kessel was a dangerous shooter—he finished his career with 413 goals—and an underrated passer who was extremely popular not only with teammates but with the fan base, perhaps because of his "everyman" appearance.

While Phil Kessel seemed enigmatic, he was a good fit with the Penguins, at least in his early years.
COURTESY OF GETTY IMAGES

APRIL 19, 2016

SULLIVAN CASTS HIS LOT WITH MATT MURRAY

MIKE SULLIVAN took an enormous risk in Game 3 of the Penguins' first-round playoff series against the New York Rangers, starting rookie goalie Matt Murray—who had zero seconds of Stanley Cup experience and had been sidelined for nearly two weeks because of a head injury—at Madison Square Garden. Sixteen saves and a 3–1 Pittsburgh victory later, Sullivan's goaltending gamble had hit the jackpot. "I don't know that any of those decisions are easy," Sullivan said. "But certainly [Murray] has played a lot of really good hockey for us." He did it in Game 3 as the youngest goalie in franchise history to make a start in the postseason, although Murray, in typical fashion, took that and almost everything else about the evening in stride. "Matt's got a real calm demeanor in there," said Sullivan, who decided to use Murray after Jeff Zatkoff had earned a split of the first two games against New York. Marc-Andre Fleury was unavailable because of a concussion.

Mike Sullivan took a high-stakes gamble when he made Matt Murray the Penguins' go-to goalie.
COURTESY OF GETTY IMAGES

JUNE 9, 2016

PERFECT SCENARIO GOES SOUR

THE PENGUINS had an increasingly difficult path to the Stanley Cup Final—they lost one game to the New York Rangers in Round 1 of the playoffs, two to Washington in Round 2, and three to Tampa Bay in Round 3—but all of their efforts through the first four games of the championship series had put them in position to do something they never had managed in three previous Cup runs: close out a title run on home ice. After locking up Cups at Chicago Stadium; the Met Center in Bloomington, Minnesota; and Joe Louis Arena in Detroit, the Penguins held a 3–1 lead in the final against San Jose heading into Game 5 at Consol Energy Center. Never mind that there was a capacity crowd inside the building eager to savor a championship; the streets and sidewalks outside of the arena were packed with an estimated 20,000 who were there to watch the game on giant screens and revel in what was about to happen. There were so many, in fact, that the Penguins announced plans to place a second giant screen in Market Square, a considerable distance from the arena, to accommodate the crowd. The Market Square screen drew a crowd estimated at 15,000. Too bad the Sharks decided to rewrite the Game 5 script, taking a 2–0 lead in the first three minutes of play and holding on for a 4–2 victory that sent the series back to San Jose for Game 6.

In 2016, the Penguins had a chance to win a Cup on home ice for the first time, but San Jose spoiled the party. COURTESY OF GETTY IMAGES

The Penguins shook off the disappointment of losing Game 5 and wrapped up their fourth Cup on the road in Game 6.
COURTESY OF GETTY IMAGES

JUNE 12, 2016

DELAYED DELIRIUM

THE PENGUINS were understandably unhappy about their failure to close out the Stanley Cup final against San Jose in Game 5 on home ice, and having to again fly across the continent to try to lock up the franchise's fourth Cup. Their motivation was obvious from the opening face-off and, unlike in Game 5, when they never had a lead, the Penguins never trailed in this one. Brian Dumoulin staked them to a 1–0 lead midway through the first period and, shortly after Logan Couture pulled the Sharks even in the second, Kris Letang scored what proved to be the Cup clincher. Patric Hornqvist hit an empty net with 62 seconds remaining in regulation to remove any doubt about the outcome and delight the estimated 16,000 fans who had gathered at Consol Energy Center to watch the game and to give the Penguins a ride back across the country that was a lot more enjoyable than the one that had taken them to northern California a few days earlier.

JANUARY 27, 2017

THE BEST OF THE BEST (MOSTLY)

WHEN THE NHL announced its list of the top 100 players in league history—its version of that list, anyway—to mark its 100th year in existence, that list would have been incomplete without a number of Penguins on it. Seven living players with ties to the organization—Mario Lemieux, Jaromir Jagr, Sidney Crosby, Ron Francis, Bryan Trottier, Paul Coffey, and Luc Robitaille—made the cut, along with late Penguins alums Tim Horton and Andy Bathgate. Notably absent from the list was Pittsburgh center Evgeni Malkin, who had seemed like a logical candidate for inclusion. "He's won two Stanley Cups [Malkin's third came a few months later], a Conn Smythe, Art Ross," Lemieux said. "It's tough." Crosby was one of just six active players to earn a spot in the top 100. "I'm just honored," he said. "It's one thing to be a part of this group, but it's a small window to play and be part of the 100th anniversary."

Evgeni Malkin was surprisingly absent from the NHL's list of its top 100 players of all time. COURTESY OF GETTY IMAGES

FEBRUARY 25, 2017

LET'S TAKE THIS OUTSIDE

OUTDOOR GAMES had pretty much lost their novelty for the Penguins by the time Philadelphia came to Heinz Field for another of them, because they had appeared in so many. Heck, even guys who were fairly new to the NHL, like young winger Jake Guentzel, had experience in them, having played in an official one while in high school in Minnesota. Perhaps that's why Guentzel, who had appeared in 22 NHL games at that point, looked so comfortable against the Flyers, turning in a strong two-way game and earning the primary assist on each of the Penguins' first two goals. Evgeni Malkin described Guentzel as "the best player on the ice," and coach Mike Sullivan noted something that would become increasingly evident as Guentzel's career progressed: "I don't think he gets overwhelmed by this type of event." Guentzel allowed that the event was "pretty special," and a teammate who appeared in his first outdoor game, goalie Matt Murray, emphasized how different it was to perform before a crowd of 67,318. "You try to treat it like just another hockey game," he said, "but in reality, it's a lot bigger stage."

Outdoors games had lost a lot of their novelty for the Penguins by the time they played their second at Heinz Field. COURTESY OF GETTY IMAGES

Chris Kunitz picked the perfect time to end a lengthy goal-scoring slump. COURTESY OF GETTY IMAGES

MAY 25, 2017

DOUBLE-OVERTIME DRAMA

NEARLY TWO decades had passed since the NHL last had a team win Stanley Cups in consecutive seasons—Detroit did it in 1997 and 1998—and the Penguins' bid to end that drought was looking precarious in Game 7 of the Eastern Conference Final against Ottawa. The Penguins and Senators had been tied at the end of regulation and still were after the first overtime. But at 5:09 of the second extra period, Chris Kunitz punched the Penguins' ticket to another Cup Final by finding a soft spot in the slot, taking a feed from Sidney Crosby, and beating Ottawa goalie Craig Anderson, who had been excellent throughout the series. "The puck fluttered off my stick," Kunitz said. "Sometimes you get lucky when you put one on net." He joined defenseman Darius Kasparaitis as the only players in franchise history to score an overtime goal in a Game 7. Oh, one other thing: Kunitz hadn't scored a goal in the previous 21 games before opening the scoring for Pittsburgh in Game 7 against the Senators.

The Penguins made it back-to-back titles by knocking off Nashville in six games in the 2017 Stanley Cup Final. COURTESY OF GETTY IMAGES

JUNE 11, 2017

CROWN 'EM AGAIN

THERE'S SOMETHING about the Penguins and Game 6 in the Stanley Cup Final. Sure, they were eliminated in one of those by the Red Wings in 2008, but they earned their first title, against Minnesota in 1991, in six, then did it again versus San Jose in 2016. So when they took a 3–2 lead into Game 6 in the 2017 final against Nashville, they had to be feeling pretty good about their chances. Turns out that things broke in their favor, but not until an evening full of suspense, because the game was 0–0 until there were just 95 seconds to go in the third period, when former Predators winger Patric Hornqvist snapped the tie and gave the Penguins a 1–0 lead. "This is where I've been playing most of my games, and to win it and score that goal here, it couldn't end any better for me," Hornqvist said. His goal was all that goalie Matt Murray, who tied Marc-Andre Fleury's franchise record with three shutouts in a playoff year, needed, but Carl Hagelin added an empty-netter with 14 seconds to play to put the finishing touches on Stanley Cup number five. Rookie left winger Jake Guentzel, who had scored 16 times in 40 regular-season games, added a playoffs-leading 13 in 25 postseason appearances. That's more than twice as many as any other Pittsburgh rookie scored in his playoff debut.

JUNE 21, 2017

A FLOWER WILTS IN PITTSBURGH

THERE WERE mixed emotions among the Penguins and their fan base in the days that followed their fifth Stanley Cup. There was predictable joy, as an estimated 650,000 people jammed the parade route to celebrate their accomplishment. At the same time, everyone was aware that Marc-Andre Fleury, one of the most beloved figures to ever pass through the organization, was on his way to Las Vegas, as GM Jim Rutherford had worked out an agreement with the Golden Knights to take Fleury instead of Matt Murray in the expansion draft. (Vegas also received a second-round draft choice for its consideration.) The decision to keep Murray was completely logical—he had just been the go-to goalie for two titles, was nine years younger, and was a lot cheaper than Fleury—but it still stung those who had grown accustomed to working alongside him, even if that meant occasionally being the victim of one of his legendary pranks. "He's the type of guy that I want in my life at all times," defenseman Brian Dumoulin said. Fleury's final act before leaving the Penguins: He personally financed a public playground in the suburb of McKees Rocks.

Longtime fan favorite Marc-Andre Fleury agreed to go to Vegas in the NHL expansion draft.
COURTESY OF GETTY IMAGES

FEBRUARY 16, 2017

HO-HUM. JUST MORE CROSBY MAGIC

SCORING AN OVERTIME winner, as Sidney Crosby did in Pittsburgh's 4–3 victory against Winnipeg at PPG Paints Arena, generally counts as a good night's work, but it was almost an afterthought for Crosby. That's because the assist he got on Chris Kunitz's goal at 6:28 of the opening period was Crosby's 1,000th point in the NHL, making him just the 86th player to reach that milestone. What made that all the more impressive was that Crosby was appearing in just his 757th game, fewer than all but 11 others who reached quadruple figures. "I was hovering around it for a while, so it's nice to get it and nice to get a win," Crosby said. Not surprisingly, Crosby deflected attention from his achievement toward those with whom he had played to that stage of his career. "I think you just reflect a bit on all the teams you've been a part of and all the guys you've played with and how quickly it goes by," he said. "I think the number itself is a nice number, but I think I probably tend to think about all the guys I've played with and all the teams I've played on." Just as predictably, his teammates were almost in awe of what they saw from him on a regular basis. "He's been a great player for every single day he's stepped foot on the ice," Kunitz said.

Sidney Crosby got to 1,000 career points in fewer games than all but 11 other NHL players. COURTESY OF GETTY IMAGES

Sidney Crosby picked up one of the few honors that had eluded him by being named MVP in the 2019 NHL All-Star Game. COURTESY OF GETTY IMAGES

JANUARY 26, 2019

CROSBY SHINES BRIGHTEST

PERHAPS HE was well-rested, because a stomach ailment kept Sidney Crosby in bed for most of the time leading up to the NHL All-Star Game competition in San Jose. Or maybe he was upset about not being able to participate in the festivities surrounding the game, including the annual skills events, and decided to take it out on the teams his Metropolitan Division squad faced in the three-on-three tournament. Whatever the reason, Crosby was a veritable force of nature, racking up four goals and four assists in two games to earn recognition as the game's MVP in voting by fans. He was the first Penguins player to receive that honor since Mario Lemieux in 1990. "I was just excited to be able to get out there, get out of the room, and exercise a bit," Crosby said. "Once I got out there, I felt better than I thought. This morning, I wasn't sure how I was going to feel, but I felt a lot better than I expected." It's safe to assume that the opponent charged with trying to do damage control against Crosby didn't share that feeling. New York Islanders forward Mathew Barzal was accustomed to seeing Crosby as a Metropolitan Division opponent, but had a different perspective as a teammate in the all-star competition. "I was literally laughing on the ice, because it was almost too easy," he said. "He was just always open, and you just hand it off to him when you're in trouble."

JANUARY 27, 2021

RUTHERFORD WALKS AWAY

O **JIM RUTHERFORD,** whose deft personnel moves helped to make the Penguins' Stanley Cup runs in 2016 and 2017 possible, abruptly resigned for "personal reasons," at least some of which were associated with restrictions imposed upon him by the COVID-19 pandemic. "It just got to a point that I decided my time was up here," he said. Rutherford was adamant that his age and health had nothing to do with his decision to leave the Penguins, and that no one above him on the corporate food chain had pushed him out. "I know everybody wants to refer to my age all the time," he said. "The guy with the toughest job in the world who just got elected [President Joe Biden] is way older than me. . . . I feel good and healthy." Rutherford firmly rejected a suggestion that someone higher up in the organization might have been responsible for shoving him out. "I really don't want to get into that," he said. "They didn't push [me] aside. As an organization, they've treated me first-class." Rutherford, whose initial association with the franchise had come as a goaltender in the 1970s, was popular inside and outside the organization. "Jim's legacy is that two Stanley Cup banners are hanging in our building and the personal relationships he's made within the organization, within the hockey world, and in the grocery store," team president David Morehouse said. Rutherford's interim replacement was his assistant GM, Patrik Allvin, but Ron Hextall was brought in as his full-time successor.

Jim Rutherford stunned the hockey world by stepping down from his position with the Penguins.
COURTESY OF GETTY IMAGES

OCTOBER 6, 2021

SULLIVAN CLAIMS THE TOP SPOT

MIKE SULLIVAN wasn't Jim Rutherford's first choice to coach the Penguins when Rutherford replaced Ray Shero as GM in 2014. Instead, Rutherford opted to give the job to Mike Johnston, who had been quite successful behind the bench with Portland in the Western Hockey League and had experience as an assistant coach in the NHL. Just a couple of months into Johnston's second year on the job, however, Rutherford decided that a change was necessary and decided to promote Sullivan, who had been coaching the Penguins' farm team in Wilkes-Barre for less than half of a season. It proved to be one of the most important and productive decisions of Rutherford's front-office tenure. Sullivan replaced Johnston in mid-December, and as summer approached, the Penguins were celebrating a Stanley Cup. Twelve months later, they did it again. Sullivan absorbed his share of criticism in the years that followed, but Rutherford and the two GMs who followed him, Ron Hextall and Kyle Dubas, never concluded that a new coach was required. Sullivan went on to become the longest-serving coach the team has ever had, and the Penguins' 5–2 victory against Chicago on this date was Sullivan's 253rd, most by any Penguins coach. "I never could have envisioned this," he said. "I couldn't be more grateful. I couldn't be more excited. I couldn't be more humbled. . . . There's been a lot of really good coaches over the history of this organization. I'm fortunate enough to be here at a time when the players are so good."

Mike Sullivan is, by many metrics, the most successful coach ever to run the Penguins' bench.
COURTESY OF GETTY IMAGES

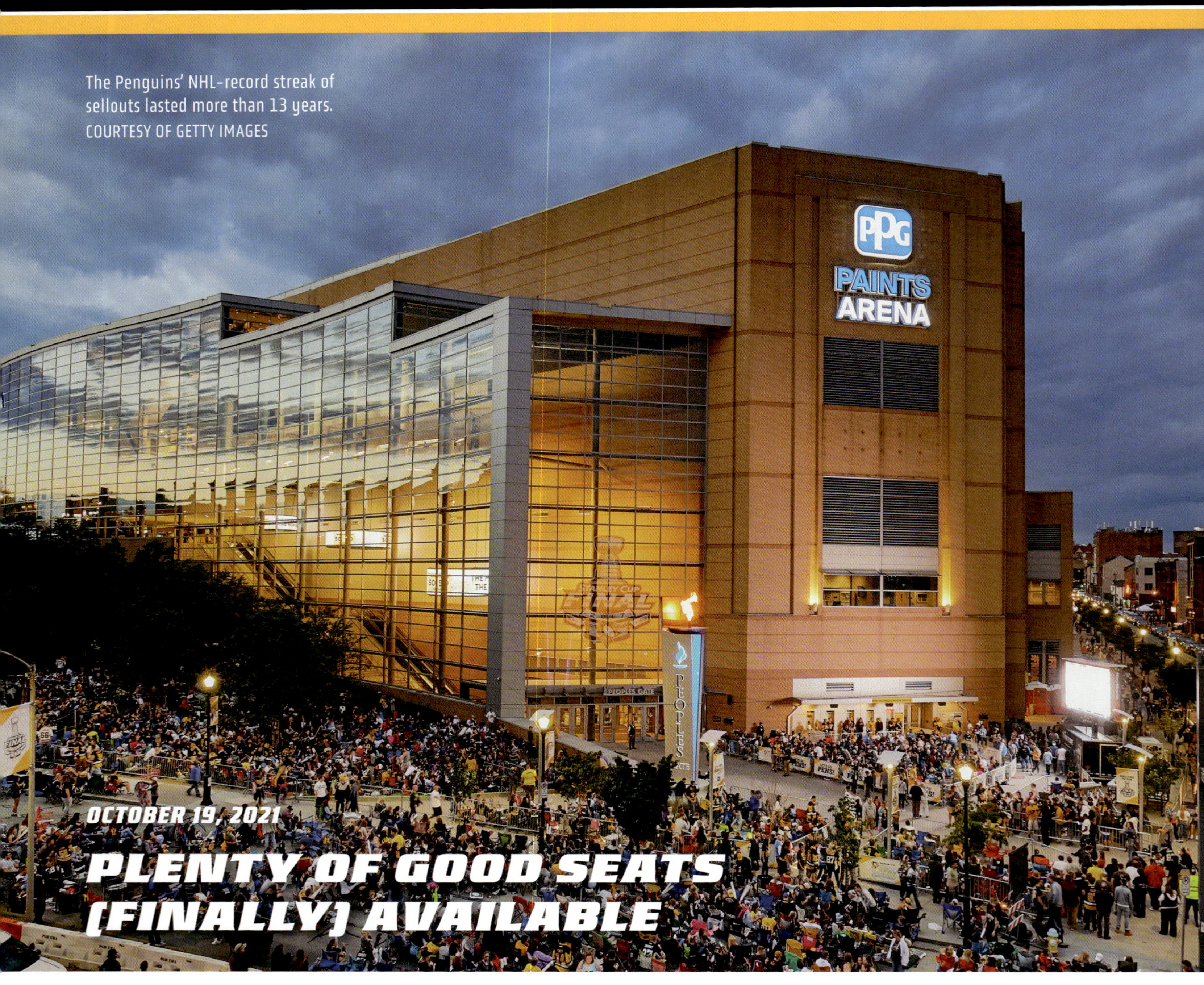

The Penguins' NHL-record streak of sellouts lasted more than 13 years. COURTESY OF GETTY IMAGES

OCTOBER 19, 2021

PLENTY OF GOOD SEATS (FINALLY) AVAILABLE

THERE WERE stretches during the Penguins' first couple of decades in the NHL—generally, at times when the team was performing as if it had just taken up competitive hockey a week or so earlier—when they would have been hard-pressed to get people to turn up for their games at gunpoint. Witness the 1983–84 season, when their average attendance was announced as 6,839 and a member of the media-relations staff acknowledged off the record a few months later that that figure had been inflated. But when the Penguins began to win games—and then championships—the turnstiles began to click regularly. The Penguins, then playing at Mellon Arena, attracted a capacity crowd to a game against Chicago on February 14, 2007, and sold out the 332 that followed until October 19, 2021, when a crowd of 16,440 turned up at PPG Paints Arena to watch the Penguins drop a 2–1 shoot-out decision to Dallas. It is considered the longest sellout streak in NHL history. Whether the Penguins could have continued to perform before full houses had there not been a pandemic will never be known, but it certainly seems possible. "If you would have told me 14 years ago you would do 14 years of sellouts, I would have said, 'No, I think you're crazy," team president David Morehouse said. "But I think our fan base proved that Pittsburgh is a hockey town. They came out and they continue to come out."

DECEMBER 9, 2021

FENWAY COMES TO PITTSBURGH

THE OWNERSHIP group headed by Mario Lemieux and Ron Burkle guided the Penguins to Stanley Cup championships in 2009, 2016, and 2017 and into a new multipurpose arena that secured the team's future in the city after acquiring the franchise out of bankruptcy in 1999. Lemieux and Burkle decided to move on, however, and sold majority interest in the team to Fenway Sports Group, whose other high-profile holdings include the Boston Red Sox and Liverpool of the English Premier League, although both men retained minority interests in the club. The sale price never was announced, but reportedly was around $900 million. "The Pittsburgh Penguins are a premier National Hockey League franchise with a very strong organization, a terrific history, and a vibrant, passionate fan base," said FSG Chairman Tom Werner. "We will work diligently to continue building on the remarkable Penguins' tradition of championships and exciting play." Werner's statement also suggested that Lemieux would continue to be heavily involved with the franchise, although that did not prove to be the case in the years that followed. "We are particularly excited to welcome Mario Lemieux and Ron Burkle to FSG and have the utmost respect for all they have done to build the Penguins into the perennially successful franchise we know today. We look forward to working with Mario, Ron, and the entire Penguins front office team."

Thomas Werner is chairman of Fenway Sports Group, which purchased a majority interest in the Penguins. COURTESY OF GETTY IMAGES

MAY 11, 2022

JACOB TROUBA TAKES OUT CROSBY

THE PITTSBURGH Penguins were holding a 3–1 lead in their first-round playoff series against the New York Rangers and had a 2–0 lead late in the second period of Game 5 at Madison Square Garden. They were controlling play and looked to be on the verge of advancing to Round 2 for the first time since 2018, in large part because of the inspired play of Sidney Crosby. But the course of the series was radically and permanently altered when New York defenseman Jacob Trouba, renowned for his penchant for delivering blows to opponents' heads, felled Crosby with an elbow or forearm in the face. Crosby left the game and did not dress for Game 6. The Penguins were predictably (and justifiably) outraged by what Trouba did— "Did you see the hit?" Penguins coach Mike Sullivan said. "Then you probably have the same opinion I do." But the NHL's Department of Player Safety disagreed, and not only declined to fine or suspend Trouba, but didn't even bother scheduling a hearing for him. Trouba certainly made it clear that he didn't believe he had done anything inappropriate, offering insights that many Penguins partisans found as easy to swallow as broken glass. "Obviously, you don't ever want to see a guy get hurt," Trouba said. "I don't know exactly what the injury is, but hopefully, it's better soon." Well, it wasn't, and Crosby wasn't cleared to rejoin the lineup until Game 7, when New York eliminated the Penguins 4–3 in overtime.

New York defenseman Jacob Trouba altered the course of the series when he delivered a head shot to Sidney Crosby. COURTESY OF GETTY IMAGES

JUNE 1, 2023

THE KYLE DUBAS ERA BEGINS

ALMOST FROM the moment that general manager Ron Hextall and president of hockey operations Brian Burke were fired shortly after the Penguins failed to qualify for the playoffs for the first time since 2006, there was speculation that Fenway Sports Group would try to pry Kyle Dubas away from Toronto, where he was GM, to replace Burke. That's exactly what happened, as Dubas joined the Penguins less than two weeks after being fired by the Maple Leafs following an apparent power struggle with team president Brendan Shanahan. "We ran a robust search," FSG executive Dave Beeston told a press conference that day. But Dubas joining the team as president of hockey operations wasn't the whole story. He not only took over the presidency but, with the blessing of his superiors in the company, also planned to serve as GM on an interim basis and would search for a full-time successor to Hextall after guiding the Penguins through the upcoming draft and free agency. (It turned out that he held the position quite a bit longer than he initially suggested he would.) He also made it clear that he believed in the potential of the Penguins' longtime core. "If people want to bet against Mike Sullivan, Sidney Crosby, Evgeni Malkin, Kris Letang, and others, they can go ahead and do so," he said. "But I'm going to bet on them and go with them here. I do think that it's a group capable of contending to win a championship."

Kyle Dubas was put in charge of every aspect of the Penguins' hockey operations.
COURTESY OF GETTY IMAGES

AUGUST 6, 2023

DUBAS TAKES A BIG SWING

THE PENGUINS have made a number of trades for future Hall of Famers over the years—Paul Coffey, Larry Murphy, Joe Mullen, and Ron Francis come immediately to mind—and Kyle Dubas didn't waste any time after taking over operation of the Penguins' front office before working out one of those. He brought in Erik Karlsson, a three-time winner of the Norris Trophy as the NHL's top defenseman, from San Jose little more than two months after assuming responsibility for guiding the organization into the future. The Penguins parted with a first-round draft choice, a second-rounder, defenseman Jan Rutta, forward Mikael Granlund, goalie Casey DeSmith, defenseman Jeff Petry, and winger Nathan Legare, in a complex three-team arrangement with the Sharks and Montreal that landed them forwards Rem Pitlick and Dillon Hamaliuk and a third-round pick in 2026, as well as Karlsson. "When it's a good player that you really want, I think that's why you spend a lot of your nights staring up at the ceiling rather than sleeping," Dubas said. "[Thinking] of different ways you can make it happen. Know the market, which other teams are going to jump in. Who can beat you to it. How they can beat you to it. How can you outdo them?" Although the move was made to maximize the Penguins' long-shot chances of contending for a Stanley Cup, Karlsson and many of his teammates did not perform to expectations and the Penguins missed postseason play for the second consecutive year.

Kyle Dubas made a high-risk, high-reward trade when he picked up defenseman Erik Karlsson from San Jose.
COURTESY OF GETTY IMAGES

OCTOBER 10, 2023

SO HAPPY TOGETHER

EVEN THE most promising and productive partnerships in pro sports tend to be rather transient. After all, there are trades and injuries and retirements that mitigate against a pair of high-profile players—let alone three of them—working on the same team for an extended period. Most high-profile players and most teams, anyway. The Penguins proved to be an exception to that rule when Sidney Crosby, Evgeni Malkin, and Kris Letang began their 18th consecutive season as teammates, making them the longest-tenured threesome in the history of North American pro sports. "It means a lot, to be honest, having the chance to win three championships with these guys," Letang said. "Been through a lot, on and off the ice, with these two guys. . . . The fact that we were always there for each other and kind of got back on our feet and kept going, it was pretty special. The fact that we were able to keep it all together, it was pretty impressive." The Penguins have won three Stanley Cups since Letang and Malkin joined Crosby for the 2006–07 season, and the team qualified for the playoffs in each of their first 16 seasons together. "When you spend that much time together and you go through the challenges and have some of the success and failure that they've been through in the years that they've been together, you become close," coach Mike Sullivan said. "I don't think anything galvanizes friendships and relationships more than when you win championships."

Sidney Crosby, Evgeni Malkin, and Kris Letang have been core members of the Penguins for years.
COURTESY OF GETTY IMAGES

NOVEMBER 30, 2023

IT'S A GOALIE GOAL

A DAY OR SO after goalie Alex Nedeljkovic scored for the Penguins' farm team in Wilkes-Barre, Tristan Jarry—who had already put a goal on his résumé while playing in the American Hockey League—was asked if he would consider trying to score one in the NHL. Jarry pretty much dismissed the notion, citing concerns about turning the puck over, or possibly causing an icing that would give the other team a favorable face-off location. "Probably not," he said. Well, Jarry was wrong. Not about the possible downside of launching a puck toward the other end of the ice, but about whether he'd be interested in trying to do it. Because when the opportunity arose during a game at Amalie Arena in Tampa, Jarry calmly tossed a puck the length of the rink, depositing it squarely in the Lightning net with 68 seconds remaining in regulation to lock up a 4–2 Penguins victory. That made him the 14th goaltender in NHL history to score a goal. (Martin Brodeur did it three times and Ron Hextall two.) "It was kind of the perfect scenario," Jarry said. "They dumped it right on net, and I didn't even have to stop it. I just shot it right on the fly, and it ended up going in."

Tristan Jarry is paid to prevent goals, but showed he can score them, too.
COURTESY OF GETTY IMAGES

DECEMBER 27, 2023

LETANG HAS LE TOUCH ON LONG ISLAND

Kris Letang came out of the NHL's holiday break in 2023 with a vengeance. COURTESY OF GETTY IMAGES

SOME TEAMS and players struggle when coming out of the NHL's annual holiday break in late December, whether it's because they had a little too much of the seasonal festivities or simply because their games got a bit out of sync after being away from the ice for a few days. Kris Letang, though, came out of the time off at full speed, assisting on six goals in the Penguins' 7–0 victory over the New York Islanders at UBS Arena on Long Island. That tied the NHL record for defensemen and made him the first guy at his position to pile up a half-dozen assists in 37-plus years. In the process, Letang also became the first NHL defenseman to account for five assists in one period. "It was pretty special," he said. "When you have a chance to play with good players, they're not the hardest plays to make. If you give it to the right guy, sometimes they score, and you get the assist." Although he was just the fourth player in franchise history to rack up six assists in a game, Letang was not the first Penguins defenseman to do it, because Ron Stackhouse pulled it off during an 8–2 victory over Philadelphia at the Civic Arena on March 8, 1975. A couple of centers, Mario Lemieux and Greg Malone, would subsequently generate six-assist games of their own. Lemieux actually did it three times during the regular season.

FEBRUARY 18, 2024

TO THE RAFTERS WITH IT

O **THERE WERE** times when Jaromir Jagr was the most beloved figure in the Penguins' organization. There also were times, like when he was on the payroll of an archrival such as Philadelphia or Washington or the New York Rangers, when much of the fan base professed to loathe him. But Jagr insisted that he never had any hard feelings toward the Penguins, who traded him to the Capitals in 2001 after it became clear that they couldn't meet his salary demands. And any animosity the public felt toward him obviously faded over the years, because the weekend when the Penguins celebrated Jagr's career—and retired his No. 68 sweater—proved to be one of the high points of the 2023–24 season. The Penguins had long planned to honor Jagr that way but had intended to put it off until he formally retired as a player. Trouble is, even though he was on the far side of 50, Jagr still hadn't hung up his skates, and Penguins officials decided there was no point in delaying it any longer. Good thing, too, because quitting wasn't in his short-term plans. "Once you're satisfied with something, you're done," Jagr said. "There always has to be a hunger to be better and better and better. That's the drive in life. I always compare myself to the Amazon jungle. If you're satisfied in the jungle, you're dead. There's no 'I'm sorry. You were good, we let you live.' No, somebody's going to eat you.' "

Jaromir Jagr became just the third player to have his number retired by the Penguins.
COURTESY OF GETTY IMAGES

Sidney Crosby separated himself from the most consistent point producers to pass through the NHL.
COURTESY OF GETTY IMAGES

APRIL 1, 2024

THIS FEAT IS A GREAT ONE

SIDNEY CROSBY has routinely tormented the New York Rangers since he entered the NHL, so perhaps it wasn't surprising when he scored two goals and set up another during a 5–2 victory at Madison Square Garden. However, his performance did more than just help the Penguins earn a couple of badly needed points in their uphill battle to secure a playoff berth in the Eastern Conference—it gave him 82 points for the season, guaranteeing that he would average at least a point per game for the 19th time, matching a feat equaled only by Wayne Gretzky. As usual, Crosby downplayed his achievement. "I knew I was getting closer," he said. "And anytime you can be in that company, it's pretty cool." Not surprisingly, his teammates were far more impressed by what Crosby has done than Crosby himself was. "It's extremely impressive," said right winger Bryan Rust, who scored the goal set up by Crosby. "To have that type of consistent impact over that many years in this league is . . . extremely special, obviously. He's in the company of only one other player, who's considered to be the best player of all time." He added that Crosby's commitment to his craft was an integral part of what he accomplished. "His work ethic is unmatched," Rust said. "He plays the game hard, works hard off the ice, works hard away from the rink. In the summertime. In the gym. Whatever. Always trying to get better."

APRIL 11, 2024

CROSBY LEADS THE WAY (AS USUAL)

On **SIDNEY CROSBY** had a goal and two assists in a 6–5 overtime victory against Detroit at PPG Paints Arena, moving him past Phil Esposito and into 10th place on the NHL's all-time points list. And that wasn't all he accomplished in this game. Crosby's assists made him the 14th player in the league to put up 1,000 of them in his career, and he did it in fewer games than all but six players. With Esposito in his rearview mirror, Crosby was able to begin closing in on the esteemed likes of Joe Sakic, Mario Lemieux, and Steve Yzerman among the league's all-time scoring leaders. "I haven't looked that closely [at the list]," Crosby said. "But to be in that company with all those players you mentioned, that means a lot. I grew up watching those players." The three points he picked up against the Red Wings helped the Penguins grab temporary possession of the second wild-card spot in the Eastern Conference playoff field. "He plays his best when the stakes are high, like all of the all-time greats that have played the game," Penguins coach Mike Sullivan said. "He's one of those guys."

Sidney Crosby's inexorable march up the NHL's all-time points list finally got him inside the top 10. COURTESY GETTY IMAGES

OCTOBER 16, 2024

TWO FOR THE RECORD BOOK

OACHIEVEMENTS THAT help to define a Hall of Fame career don't come along very often, and they almost never occur for teammates in the same game. Then again, Sidney Crosby and Evgeni Malkin aren't most teammates. They were, for years, the most potent one-two punch at center in the NHL, and as their careers are winding down they continue to make magic and memories, even if it doesn't happen as often as it did when they were younger. Crosby was the first to reach his personal milestone, setting up a Bryan Rust goal in the first period of a 6–5 overtime victory against Buffalo to become just the 10th player in league history to accumulate 1,600 points. He didn't stop there, though. At 3:26 of the third period, Crosby set up Malkin for his 500th goal in the NHL, making him the 48th player in the league to score that many. "It's a great story. Sid passed to me," said Malkin who, coincidentally enough, had assisted on Crosby's 500th goal. "It's like, amazing. I love it." There was, indeed, a lot for him to like about that goal, which he scored while lying on his stomach after taking a between-the-legs pass from Crosby, who was behind the Sabres' goal line. "The way he did it, that was a pretty awesome goal," Crosby said. "I'll have a great memory of that one."

Sidney Crosby and Evgeni Malkin have teamed up to do a lot of great things during their careers. COURTESY GETTY IMAGES

JANUARY 2, 2025

SIDNEY CROSBY: MAN OF THE CENTURY

SOME EXTRAORDINARY players have passed through the NHL during the past quarter century. Connor McDavid and Alex Ovechkin. Cale Makar and Patrick Kane. Nathan MacKinnon and Nicklas Lidstrom. And a whole lot more. Enough that it might be necessary someday to add a wing to the Hockey Hall of Fame

Sidney Crosby was cited as the top player in the first quarter of this century. COURTESY OF GETTY IMAGES

just to accommodate all of the worthy entrants who played during the 2000s. Sportsnet, a Canadian TV network, took on the daunting challenge of selecting the top 25 players who have performed in the league since the turn of the century, with a heavy emphasis on what they accomplished after 1999. (That explains why, say, Penguins alum Jaromir Jagr, who broke into the NHL in 1990 and played there until the 2017–18 season, didn't make the cut.) The final rankings were sure to provoke some heated discussions—that's probably exactly what the network had in mind when it decided to take on the challenge of putting the list together—but it's unlikely that many objective observers had a problem with Sidney Crosby holding down the number one spot.

JANUARY 17, 2025

GOALIE GOAL, REDUX

IT'S STILL fairly rare for goaltenders to score a goal, although it has become far more common in recent years. Alex Nedeljkovic of the Penguins joined the club of those who have done it in the NHL, but his accomplishment to cap a 5–2 victory at KeyBank Center in Buffalo came with a couple of unprecedented wrinkles: He became the first NHL goalie to score in a game in which he also received an assist, and he established himself as the only goaltender to get a goal in the NHL, American Hockey League, and ECHL, the top three rungs of professional hockey in North America. Nedeljkovic scored after the Sabres, trying to overcome a two-goal deficit, had replaced goalie Ukko-Pekka Luukkonen with an extra attacker. He launched a shot that settled into the empty net in the Sabres' end of the ice at 17:18 of the third period. "Anytime we have a lead like that, a two- or three-goal lead, I was thinking about [trying to score]," Nedeljkovic said. "I might have been thinking a little too much about it when they pulled him at first with five minutes left, but I settled down after that. The guys did a good job of clearing out the middle, all going to the right spots. I wasn't too sure it was going to make it out of the zone, let alone go all the way down, so this is pretty exciting."

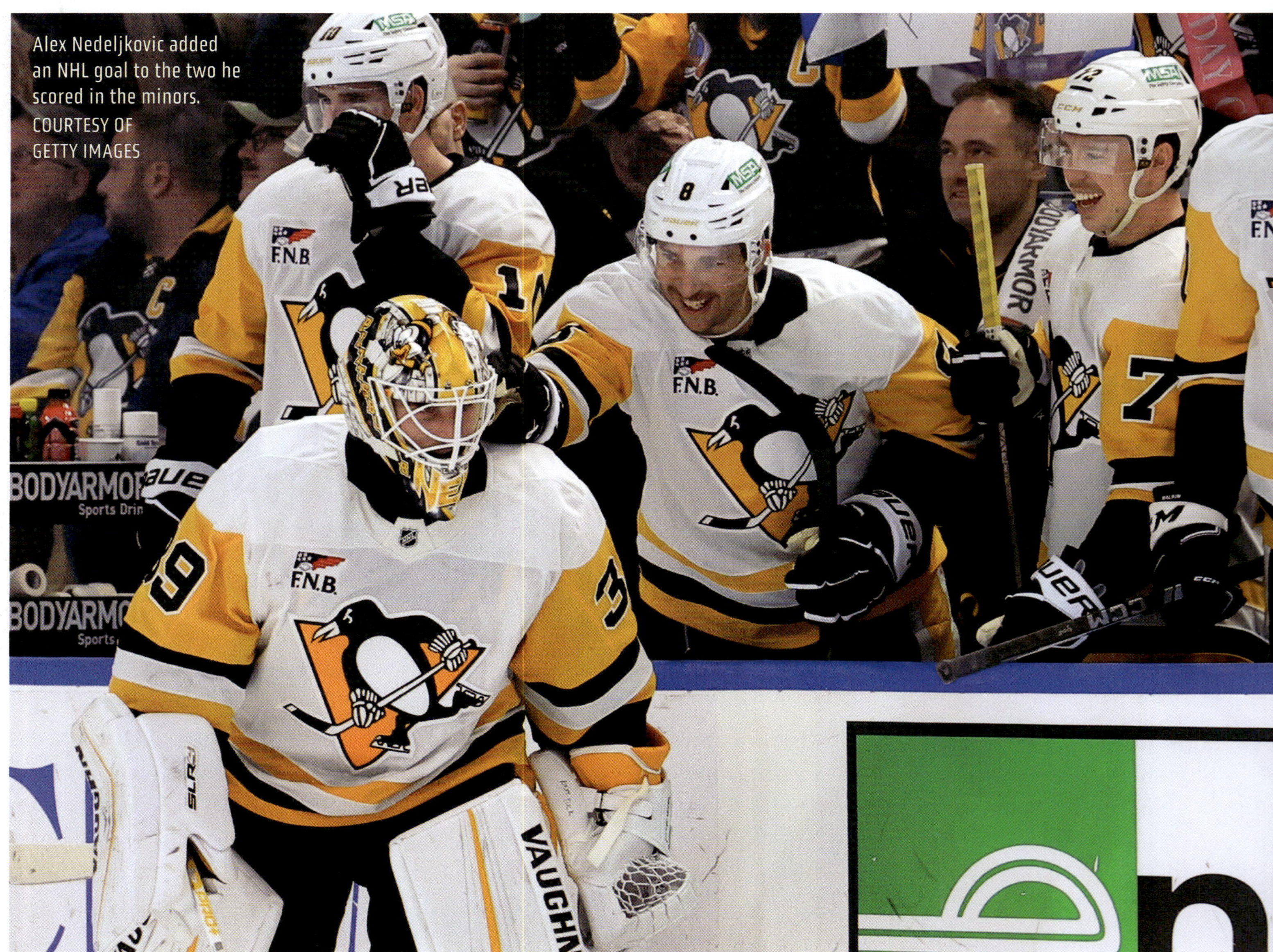

Alex Nedeljkovic added an NHL goal to the two he scored in the minors. COURTESY OF GETTY IMAGES

Longtime play-by-play man Mike Lange was one of the most significant off-ice figures in Penguins history.
COURTESY OF GETTY IMAGES

FEBRUARY 19, 2025

PITTSBURGH LOSES ANOTHER LEGEND

MIKE LANGE wasn't just a Hockey Hall of Fame play-by-play man or a guy who did Penguins broadcasts for the better part of five decades. He was, at times, the virtual face of the franchise and probably had a more profound effect on it than any other off-ice figure, including GMs and team presidents. His uncanny feel for the game and his personable nature pulled in fans when the team he covered really couldn't, and he kept them there by being entertaining and informative. Along the way, he developed numerous catch phrases that became synonymous with him. Almost any Pittsburgh fan who appreciated his work—which is to say, any Pittsburgh fan who followed the team from the mid-1970s, when he joined the Penguins after a stint with the San Diego Gulls of the Western Hockey League, until he retired in 2021—could recite them on command. "He's smiling like a butcher's dog." "He doesn't know whether to cry or wind his watch." And, of course, the one he used to punctuate any Pittsburgh victory: "Ladies and gentlemen, Elvis has left the building." Lange, 76 when he passed away, was a native of Sacramento, but he formed an enduring bond with the people of Western Pennsylvania. He didn't just speak to them; he became one of them. Aside from one year away from the Penguins—when the team had gone into bankruptcy in 1975—Lange was an unwavering presence in Pittsburgh. Managements changed and players moved on, but Lange was a constant. In addition to everything else, he mentored guys like Josh Getzoff and Steve Mears, who eventually would take their place behind a microphone at Penguins games. His passing left a void in the Pittsburgh hockey community that will not be filled for many years, if ever.

SOURCES

INDEX